Ann-Sofie Dahl

US Policy in the Nordic-Baltic Region

During the Cold War and after

Santérus
Academic Press
Sweden

www.santerus.se

All rights reserved. No part of this publication may be reproduced, stored in a retrieval system, or transmitted, in any form or by any means, electronic, mechanical, photocopying, recording, or otherwise, without the prior written permission of the publisher, except in the case of brief quotations embodied in critical articles and reviews.

© 2008 Ann-Sofie Dahl and Santérus Academic Press Sweden
ISBN 978-91-7335-009-9
Layout: Harnäs Text
Cover profile: Sven Bylander
Cover artwork: *Creation of the World X* from 1906
by the Lithuanian artist Mikalojus Ciurlionis (Source: WikiPaintings)
Santérus Academic Press is an imprint of
Santérus Förlag, Stockholm, Sweden
academicpress@santerus.se
Printed by BOD, Norderstedt, Germany

Contents

ACKNOWLEDGMENTS

1. INTRODUCTION 9
   1.1 US Policy and Nordic-Baltic Security 9

   PART I THE UNITED STATES AND
   THE NORDIC REGION DURING THE COLD WAR

2. THE NORDIC REGION IN MILITARY CONTAINMENT 19
   2.1 The strategy of Containment in Scandinavia 19
   2.2 Subregions in the North 20
   2.3 The early years 24
   2.4 "Keep them strong" 28
   2.5 From massive retaliation to maritime strategy 30

3. THE NORDIC REGION IN IDEOLOGICAL CONTAINMENT 36
   3.1 Solid democracies in the West 36
   3.2 Neutrality and NATO conditions 37
   3.3 Deterrence and détente 41
   3.4 Footnotes 42
   3.5 "Keep them friendly" 46
   3.6 Moral superpowers in the North 48
   3.7 Innocent Nordic countries 52

PART II THE NORDIC-BALTIC REGION IN UNIPOLAR STRATEGY

4. THE NORDIC-BALTIC REGION IN UNIPOLAR STRATEGY: PART I (1991–1996) — 57

4.1 Subregions in the North — 57
4.2 The first phase: benevolent lack of interest (1991–1993) — 61
    4.2.1 Regional instability — 61
4.3 The second phase: a Baltic dilemma (1994–1997) — 65
    4.3.1 A gray zone — 65
    4.3.2 Regionalization of security — 68
    4.3.3 Intra-Nordic rivalries — 72

5. THE NORDIC-BALTIC REGION IN UNIPOLAR STRATEGY: PART II (1997–2007) — 79

5.1 The third phase: unipolar determination (1997–1998) — 79
    5.1.1 The Nordic-Baltic region post-Madrid — 79
    5.1.2 Northern and Baltic initiatives — 80
5.2 The fourth phase: preparing a second round of enlargement (1999–2002) — 83
    5.2.1 A change of mood — 83
    5.2.2 The two nonaligned Nordic countries — 86
    5.2.3 Bush II and the Baltic issue — 88
5.3 The fifth phase: a new security system in the Nordic-Baltic region (2002–2007) — 91

6. THE NORDIC-BALTIC REGION AND THE UNIPOLAR VALUES — 93

6.1 Nordic bandwagoning and "Europeanization" — 93
6.2 The transatlantic link — 95
6.3 September 11, 2001 – and Iraq, 2003 — 98

7. CONCLUSION — 102

7.1 The Nordic region in US strategy during bipolarity — 102
7.2 The Nordic-Baltic region in US strategy in the post-Cold War era — 104

BIBLIOGRAPHY — 107

Acknowledgments

This book has greatly benefited from numerous conversations, interviews, and comments from colleagues and practitioners on both sides of the Atlantic. In particular part II draws to a large extent on interviews conducted over the years that this project has been in progress. Special thanks to Ingemar Dörfer, Kjeld Hillingsø, Pauli Järvenpää, and Rolf Tamnes for taking the time to read the manuscript in a final version, and for sharing their insights and advice; this book is all the better for their comments and suggestions. I am truly grateful for the generous funding that the project received from Tekn. dr Marcus Wallenbergs Stiftelse för utbildning i internationellt industriellt företagande (The Dr. Marcus Wallenberg Scholarship Foundation for Education in International Industrial Entrepreneurship), and for the support provided by the Swedish Foreign Ministry, the National Defence College, Letterstedtska Stiftelsen, and Magn. Bergvalls Stiftelse.

1. Introduction

This study is an analysis of the strategic and political relationship between the Nordic – and later Nordic-Baltic – region and the United States, as it evolved from the beginning of the Cold War and during the first 15 years of the unipolar era. What has been the position of the region in the overall strategy of the US in the 60 years since the end of World War II? How has the US, unilaterally and as the major NATO ally, viewed the strategic and political situation in the Nordic – and from the end of the Cold War, the Nordic-Baltic-region – during this period of time?

How has the transatlantic strategic and political relationship evolved over time, and what direction is it likely to take in the years and decades to come? How, and in what way, has US policy toward the region been affected by the dramatic changes in the international order during this period – and vice versa? What role will the region play in future US policy, as this becomes increasingly preoccupied with concerns and regional problems of a very different nature to those that have dominated developments during the past 50 or 60 years?

1.1 US Policy and Nordic-Baltic Security

The region surrounding the Baltic Sea has seen enormous changes in its security structures in a short period of time, historically speaking. In the words of a foreign minister, the Baltic Sea has gone from being a "barrier of water, which divided nations and people, to a Sea of Peace" since the end of the Cold War.[1] Nowhere is the transformation of the region and

---

[1] Speech by Carl Bildt, CBSS Foreign Minister meeting, Malmö, June 12, 2007.

the international system from a bipolar to a unipolar world more striking than in the destiny of the three Baltic countries – locked behind the Iron Curtain as Soviet Republics after World War II, and sovereign members of the Western defense alliance a half-century later. In other ways, the security system of the region comes across as more static. Though surrounded on all sides, except on the Russian border, by NATO allies, and in spite of close military and political cooperation with NATO, Finland and Sweden have maintained their nonaligned security doctrines in the new system.

There are also other reminders of the past. During the presidency of Vladimir Putin, the world has witnessed a troubling return of Russian assertiveness toward the Baltic and other neighboring countries. The debacle surrounding the removal of a statue in Estonia in May 2007, with Russian-instigated riots and a blockade of the Estonian embassy in Moscow, confirmed the view that Moscow has yet to accept the sovereignty of the former Soviet republics even after three years of Baltic membership in NATO. The Russian tendency to bully its neighbors is also evident in the use of trade sanctions and other forms of pressure, primarily in the field of energy supply, which has emerged as the number one foreign policy instrument used by the Putin government. Of particular worry to the region is the Russian–German gas pipeline planned to run through the Baltic Sea, and which Russia claims will need to be defended by an enlarged Baltic Sea fleet. Trends in Putin's Russia are indeed "troubling," as American Secretary of State Condoleezza Rice put it in the spring of 2007; especially so for the small countries bordering on the former superpower.

Even so, regional developments have been nothing short of spectacular in the past decades. In retrospect, one could even argue that it was there, in the very northernmost corner of Europe, that the design of the future security system was determined after the fall of the Berlin Wall. The inclusion of the former Soviet republics in the unipolar security system posed a number of challenges for that system and its main actors. How the West should handle this new step was a hotly contested issue at the top of the agenda for years after the bipolar collapse. Although in many ways of marginal importance and geographically distant to the unipolar power, the new Nordic-Baltic region emerged as key to the stability of a much wider – perhaps even global – area.

However, for a long time after the end of the Cold War, Baltic membership in NATO was far from certain. The general attitude in Washington, toward the emerging region was for years characterized by a sense of benevolent neglect. Several years into the 1990s, attempts to interview US policy-makers on the subject of Nordic-Baltic security basically met with polite inquiries about the relevance of studying something so utterly lacking in political and military interest.

As viewed in Washington, the Baltic Sea region was at this point still seen as being made up solely of the peaceful and stable Nordic countries. It would take another few years before the countries on both sides of the Sea merged into one analytical entity in US policy, as they were already in the minds of the regional actors themselves before the end of the Cold War. For quite some time, much energy was invested to avoid such an outcome, not only in Moscow but also even within the Alliance. The region consisting of the three Baltic States was long seen in the American capital as an extremely sensitive issue, as an area where an emerging "gray zone" could present the US with severe difficulties and, in a worst-case scenario, pose a major threat to world stability.

Neither the US nor NATO were ready or willing to commit at this point. Also, seemingly more urgent matters, such as developments in the Balkans, dominated the political scene in Washington, to the point where other parts of the world risked American neglect. In addition, the fragile relationship with Moscow was a main concern of US policy at this time, a policy pursued even at the expense of vulnerable actors such as the Baltic States.

The regional actors themselves did not share the American view of the region as in no particular need of attention or action. Quite the contrary: from a Nordic perspective, the end of the bipolar era was not perceived as an exclusively positive development in terms of security. Of course, the Nordic countries (Sweden, Denmark, Norway, Finland, and Iceland) wholeheartedly celebrated the liberation and democratization of the neighboring states, which had finally been released from the iron grip of the former Soviet bloc. But while toasting the breakdown of the Cold War era, they were also in a position to witness the simultaneous deterioration of their own strategic situation as the bipolar system – hardly politically attractive but definitely strategically stable – was replaced by an increased level of instability and insecurity in their own region. In the words of one scholar, the Nordic countries were experiencing a heavy dose of "Cold War nostalgia."[2]

The combination of a significantly increased level of instability east of the region, and what appeared as a highly uncertain future commitment to European – and in particular North European – security by the sole remaining superpower, created a sense of urgency, isolation, and concern among the countries in the North in the early years of the unipolar order.

2   Waever 1992.

In the Nordic region as elsewhere, many established patterns and structures were rearranged as the international system moved from bipolarity to unipolarity. NATO's three Nordic allies – Denmark, Norway, and Iceland – watched uneasily as their main partner, the United States, packed up the bulk of its belongings. It left behind a reduced military presence in Europe, an uncertain military commitment, and a group of concerned allies.

Ever since the end of the Cold War, all five Nordic countries have strongly expressed the view that protection and support must, and can only, arrive from the United States in one form or the other. That view represented a clear break with the rhetorical traditions of the past. However, ever since the collapse of the bipolar system, the Nordic countries have had to deal with the uncertainties surrounding the US interest in playing such a protective role in a new world order lacking a hostile rival superpower to the east of the Baltic Sea. Especially in the early phases of the new and unipolar world, the commitment of the United States to such a role, and the capacity to maintain it, were seen as highly uncertain, as was the strength and depth of US engagement in Europe generally.

During the Cold War, the security policies of the Nordic region had formed a colorful quilt of strategic models, referred to as the Nordic balance. The regional strategic models ranged from NATO membership without national forces of its own but with US troops stationed on its territory (Iceland); to preconditioned Alliance participation with no NATO forces or equipment on their ground in peacetime (Denmark and Norway); to self-imposed official nonalignment combined with a secret scheme of cooperation with NATO (Sweden); and finally, to a doctrine of nonalignment imposed upon the country by an unfortunate set of geopolitical and strategic circumstances (Finland).

For all the remaining differences in official security doctrines, the five Nordic countries come across as strikingly homogeneous in their strategic conclusions a few years into the new millennium. The two nonaligned Nordic countries, Sweden and Finland, opted to maintain their doctrines in the post-Cold War world. Nevertheless, they found it necessary to revise their security agendas, in which official emphasis on the significance of the transatlantic link was promoted to a top priority. When the two countries voted on the issue of membership in the European Union in the fall of 1994, security concerns played a key role for the outcome of the Finnish vote in favor of such membership, but hardly mattered at all in the Swedish case.

The two neighbors also embarked on parallel strategies to enhance cooperation with NATO through active participation in the Partnership for Peace program initiated in 1994, and by providing troops to serve under NATO command in the IFOR, SFOR, and KFOR contingents in Bosnia and Kosovo, and later in the ISAF in Afghanistan. After half a century of intricate political balancing between the two blocs, there could no longer be any doubt about the Swedish and Finnish position in the West.

Since Iceland and Norway have opted to stay out of the EU, Denmark remains the only Nordic country to hold dual membership in both the EU and NATO, although in both cases conditioned by restrictions. The three EU members are all loyal members of the Union and officially supportive of the efforts to develop the European security and defense policy, but in no way do they consider the EU capable of compensating for an American presence in Europe. All Nordic EU members have, albeit with varying emphasis, objected to the proposals which regularly emanate from the Continent to replace the US with an independent European military force, or with a system of double structures. That is a project they all consider unnecessary, disruptive, and very unlikely to succeed. Jointly and separately, the two nonaligned Nordic countries have emerged as forceful advocates within the EU and in their roles as partners to NATO in peacekeeping and crisis management; areas in which they have themselves traditionally demonstrated great expertise. In the mid-1990s, these areas were included in the expanded NATO security agenda, and also adopted by the EU under the heading of the "Petersburg tasks."

For Atlanticist NATO ally Norway, Europe was revisited in the early 1990s as a possible venue to increase North European security, as the US turned its strategic attention elsewhere. However, Norway risked further marginalization when a second referendum on EU membership in 1994 resulted in the same outcome as an earlier vote in 1974, when membership was first rejected by the Norwegian electorate. Nevertheless, Norway's strategic value remained unchallenged by its unique position as the only NATO country with a border with Russia until Baltic accession to NATO in 2002. The long coastline on the Atlantic is another valuable strategic asset for the country.

The process leading up to the first round of NATO enlargement in the post-Cold war world to three new countries, which in addition were former members of the Warsaw Pact, resulted in a renewed focus on the strategic situation in the very north of Europe. The three small and vulnerable Baltic States, excluded in that first round, were beginning to fear that their destiny was in a vague and strategically uncertain gray zone. The sense of strategic urgency already felt by the Baltic states was further amplified by the opinion expressed in the early 1990s by a number of security experts in the Pentagon and at NATO HQ, that the three countries bordering on Russia were basically "indefensible."

For the Nordic countries, the concerns voiced by their Baltic neighbors only served to demonstrate the strategic significance of their common, extended, region, and the urgent need for external involvement from the West. Some – academics and practitioners alike – saw the reshaping of the European map as evidence of an increased tendency toward a *regionalization* of security. Such a scenario was, however, not welcomed with great enthusiasm on either side of the Baltic Sea. Not only would such a development, it was feared, hand the Nordic countries (of which two were nonaligned) a significant amount of strategic responsibility toward the Baltic countries, for which they were neither militarily nor mentally prepared. But the basic idea of regionalization also seemed to exclude an American role of any significance in the region, instead placing the burden of military support for the Baltic countries on more or less unwilling and inadequately equipped regional shoulders.

A burst of new and energized US policy toward Europe at the end of the decade tempered some of the regional feelings of abandonment. A bipartisan task force sponsored by the US Council on Foreign Relations in 1999 concluded that the region had rapidly moved to a position as a "focal point of US policy."[3] Even so, key questions still remained to be addressed on the permanence of US engagement. One such central question concerned the degree of institutionalization of US policy toward the Baltic States. Could the US now be considered a player in the Nordic-Baltic region on a more permanent basis? How dependent was the policy pursued on the personal interest displayed for Nordic-Baltic issues by a number of Clinton Administration officials and political appointees at the State Department? What role would the Nordic-Baltic region have in the new millennium, and how would it fit with the political agenda brought to Washington by the Bush II presidency?

These concerns were quickly overturned by the new administration. Things improved quite dramatically from a Baltic perspective as NATO moved toward a second round of enlargement, and the European Union slowly moved toward its first wave of new membership of former Eastern bloc countries in the post-Cold War era. As new threats of fundamentalist terrorism with a global impact would soon take control of the foreign policy agenda, the expansion of NATO started in the late 1990s was concluded during the Bush II presidency with a spectacular "big bang" with seven new members, including the three former Soviet republics in the Baltic region. The Prague Summit in the fall of 2002, when the Baltic countries were invited to start negotiations on NATO membership, was a strong

---

3   Brzezinski and Larrabee 1999, p. v.

manifestation of the genuine feelings of commitment in Washington toward Nordic-Baltic security in the 21st century.

As a result of the enlargement processes, both NATO and the EU now faced a range of new neighbors to the East – the Ukraine, Moldova, Belarus, apart from Russia – and in the Southeast, the republics of Southern Caucasus. With new neighbors and new borders, political and economic instability again moved closer to both organizations. And with daunting problems in the new regional "near abroad," the actors in the Baltic Sea region may have a special role to play, sharing their special insights and experiences with the vulnerable countries on the opposite side of the fence, Considering this situation, and with energy supplies bursting onto the security agenda as a top concern, it would indeed make sense to keep at least "a modest degree of the strategic attention of the United States focused on this (Nordic-Baltic) region."[4] With several missions of a highly urgent nature demanding US attention elsewhere, it is however far from certain that this will indeed be the case to a sufficient extent.

This study analyzes US policy toward the regional actors, and the strategic and political relationship between the superpower and the Nordic-Baltic region, during the bipolar as well as the unipolar years. During the 50 years of Cold War when the Baltic countries were locked up in Soviet custody, the analytical focus of the study is on the countries of the Nordic region. It is expanded to include the three Baltic States as they become an integral part of the regional security pattern in the post-Cold War era. The study thus takes a broad perspective, discussing US policy and the relationship with the regional actors from the end of World War II, throughout the Cold War, and during the first, often tumultuous, 15 years of the post-Cold War world. How has this relationship evolved over time? To what extent, and how, has that relationship and US policy toward the region been affected by developments in the international system?

Inspired by the dual perspective which characterized the US grand strategy of Containment, the analysis is divided into two parts: Nordic-Baltic location in US policy from a *geopolitical* perspective, and from an *ideological* perspective. Barry Buzan makes a similar distinction of the *essential structure* of a security structure between what he refers to as the *distribution of power* (geopolitics) and the *level and pattern of enmity and amity* (ideological relations) among the members of a *security complex*.[5] Such a division makes analytical sense also in the world after 1989. Containment is no longer the main security policy instrument of the US, but friendship and animosity

---

4 Asmus, quoted in Dörfer 2005.
5 Buzan 1991, p. 196 ff.

remain key dimensions when defining political relations, as are geopolitical considerations departing from military and strategic observations.

Security in the Nordic and Nordic-Baltic region has always attracted quite a limited following, which is reflected in the relatively short supply of scholarly studies in the field. Most of these have approached security from a purely regional or national perspective, discussing issues such as the Nordic balance, the regional and national merits of nonalignment versus alignment, and so on. While this study has benefited from all earlier works, some have proven of particular value. One example is Norwegian historian Rolf Tamnes' study of the High North; another the dissertation by Charles Silva on the role of Scandinavia in US military planning in the crucial first years after World War II. For both periods, Swedish scholar Ingemar Dörfer has provided a number of insightful studies on Nordic security. For the unipolar years, the work by Ron Asmus individually and with his former colleagues at RAND is of course central to any discussion, also because of the political impact these studies had on the practical course of US policy.

PART I.
THE UNITED STATES AND THE NORDIC REGION DURING THE COLD WAR

2. The Nordic Region in Military Containment

2.1 The strategy of Containment in Scandinavia

In his "long telegram," George Kennan pointed in February, 1946 to a range of problems from which, as he saw it, US policy was suffering, and suggested instead a new direction of policy based less on negotiations and concessions and more on political and military strength. The new policy that resulted from the critical analysis presented by Kennan – the grand strategy of *Containment* – was of relevance also to the northern part of Europe. As the foundation for US bipolar strategy throughout the Cold War, Containment dealt both with the ideological threat generated by the Soviet Union as well as the geopolitical and military consequences of the bipolar situation.[6] From a military perspective, the bipolar conflict was approached at three basic levels: the Continental perspective with the dominant Central Front; the Maritime Perspective; and the Strategic-Nuclear Perspective.[7] How did the Nordic region fit into the Containment strategy? How did this strategy apply to the Nordic region? What was the military role and position of this region and its various parts (or sub-regions) during the bipolar years?

---

6 Gaddis 1982, pp. 19 ff.
7 Tamnes 1991, pp. 18–31.

2.2 Subregions in the North

The strategy of Containment departed from the defense of the *Eurasian rim land,* with the Central Front as its main focus. As a result of this concentration of strategic interest on the heartland of Europe, the northern part of the Continent occupied quite a peripheral position in Containment policy.[8] Especially in the first Cold War period, the Nordic region was seen as a distant *flank* to the main area of interest located in the central parts of Europe. This was particularly true in NATO analysis, with its main focus on the Central Front throughout the Cold War years.[9] The superpower perspective of the United States at times resulted in a different view of the strategic role of the North than that which prevailed at NATO HQ. In US policy, the Nordic region was primarily approached from its geographic location *between* the two superpowers, whose strategic air routes passed straight over the very northern part of the region. In this context, the Nordic region was thus not primarily seen as a distant area of minor strategic significance, but one with a crucial location next door to the rival superpower. This mirrors the dual role of the US, as one of two main players in the bipolar superpower game while also a partner (although indeed the dominant one) in the Western alliance. Pursuing the two roles in tandem was not always without complications.

Regions can be divided into *subregions:* the Nordic region consisted not of one, but a number of strategic subregions during the Cold War. In this study, a subregion could be either strategic/military or political/ideological, or both when the two coincide.[10] The multiplicity of Cold War strategic subregions was a result of, but also underlines the diversity of, geographic and geopolitical realities within the region. Consequently, the various subregions in the Cold War period were of different strategic value to the US. In addition, this value fluctuated over the years both within the main region and within the overall strategy of Containment.

The "High North" has often been understood as basically the equivalent of the "Northern Flank," although in reality, it was only one of several Cold War subregions. This area consisted primarily of Northern Norway, and, implicitly if not explicitly, also covered the rough northern parts of nonaligned Sweden and Finland. At this northernmost tip of the region, the two superpowers found themselves in close physical contact, literally speaking only yards apart through the border that NATO ally Norway shared with the Soviet Union. The main center of the High North was

---

8   See Tamnes 1991, for example p. 24.
9   Ibid, p. 137; Myers 1979, p. 162; SOU 1994, p. 112.
10 Cf. Knudsen and Neumann 1995.

located around the Arctic and Barents areas, and the subregion was defined by the geographic proximity to strategically central parts on the Soviet side such as the Kola Peninsula.

Three additional strategic subregions could be identified during the bipolar period. One, confronted by an entirely different strategic reality to the concerns occupying the High North and the Northern Flank, covered the area of Denmark, Southern Norway, and Southern Sweden, with the Baltic Straits and the narrow waters of Öresund as its strategic center. This southern subregion received its main strategic significance from its geographic proximity to the Central Front and the European mainland. The territorial attachment of Jutland and the region of Schleswig-Holstein to the Continent made Denmark a crucial front-line state in Alliance strategy throughout the Cold War.

The East German documents analyzed by Carl-Axel Gemzell at Copenhagen University reveal how Soviet-led troops regularly trained for a large-scale invasion of the Danish islands and mainland right up until the very last days of the Cold War (and even thereafter).[11] The documents from the East German archives also show the Warsaw Pact planning for a nuclear attack on the densely populated Copenhagen area at an early stage of a bipolar conflict. The study shocked the Danish public when first published in the mid-1990s. And while it is evident that "(e)ver since the formation of NATO, it has attached considerable importance to the Danish Straits," [12] the strong reactions to Gemzell's report suggest that not even the military in the West was entirely up to date on the role of nuclear arms in Warsaw Pact planning, or that such weapons were intended for the Danish capital early in a bipolar conflict.[13]

The burden placed on the inadequately prepared Danish military to control these Exits was particularly heavy in the years prior to West German rearmament in 1957–1958, and the creation of the NATO BALTAP command. This event provoked the 1961 "note crisis" when the Soviet Union protested against an increased West German presence in the Baltic Sea.[14] As a non-NATO member, Sweden did not find itself within the realms of Article Five protection. Nevertheless, Southern Sweden was tacitly included under the military auspices of the Danish air force as a result of the nonaligned country's location on the shores of the strategically crucial

---

11 See the special report on "Danmark som slagmark" in *Berlingske Tidende*, 23 February 1997; Gemzell 1996 and 1998; and Hillingsø 2004, pp. 177 ff. and Chapter 6.
12 Ausland 1986, p. 115.
13 Hillingsø 2004, p. 191.
14 Petersen 1987, p. 20.

Baltic Exits, where it was key for NATO to maintain military control in order to deny the Soviet Union and its allies exit from the Baltic Sea.[15]

The Atlantic part of the Nordic region, with Iceland and Greenland and the long coastline of Norway, formed another, third, subregion. Its prime strategic value was in the protection of the Atlantic Sea Lanes, a task that however was also extended to the southern part of Norway, and to some extent the Danish mainland, as a consequence of the responsibilities attached to guarding the Baltic Exits. As "stepping stone" areas between the continents, the Atlantic subregion provided territory for fueling stops for the United States air force on eastbound missions, and bases for American aircraft and vessels on Greenland and Iceland. In the very early years of the postwar period, before the Western world realized the full scope of Soviet expansionism, this was the only subregion capable of evoking any major American interest in the North. Great efforts were made from the beginning of the Cold War to secure the safety of Greenland. The possession of Greenland was actually a key factor behind the American interest in including Denmark in the Alliance. Referring to the unimpressive state of the Danish military after the war, Petersen remarks that in this early phase of the Cold War, "Denmark proper was generally considered indefensible and a military liability, rather than an asset" for NATO.[16] Greenland was also a major reason for Denmark's decision to join NATO, since US assistance was vital for the defense of the massive island.[17]

As part of its "a la carte" membership in NATO, with a number of conditions restricting its obligations and participation in the Alliance, Denmark had made clear that there would be no air bases and no nuclear weapons deployed on Danish territory in peacetime.[18] No such restrictions however applied to Greenland. The 1951 bilateral agreement with the US allowed for the establishment of air bases and "virtually unlimited military activity" on Greenland, but on the subject of nuclear weapons, the text was vague and ambiguous, neither admitting nor denying their existence. This secretive practice was interrupted in 1968, when the Danish government was forced to address the issue after an accident involving a US B-52 carrying nuclear weapons at the Thule airbase in Greenland.[19]

15   For accounts of the extensive contacts which nonaligned Sweden maintained with NATO during the Cold War, see SOU 1994:11; also Dahl 1999a.
16   Petersen 1987, p. 17. Cf. Tamnes 1991, pp. 29. On Danish preparedness in the early years, see Moores 2002.
17   Honkanen 2002a, p. 40.
18   On membership "a la carte", Dörfer 1986.
19   Villaume 1999, p. 32, Honkanen 2002a, pp. 42–45. For a detailed account, see the DUPI-report *Grønland under den kolde krig* (1997).

In addition to the US presence on Greenland, the Danish government also accepted a navigation installation on the Færø Islands in the 1960s. Similar facilities had been constructed in Northern Norway where the US Strategic Air Command had been given landing access, and invited to station equipment and some ground personnel in 1952. Facilities for storing nuclear weapons were built in both countries, in spite of the strict conditions placed on their NATO membership.[20] Both Scandinavian NATO countries insisted on restrictions with regards to military exercises in areas sensitive to the Soviet Union – Finnmark in the very north of Norway, and on the Danish island of Bornholm, located south of the Swedish coast in the Baltic Sea.[21]

Finally, a fourth Cold War subregion consisted of Sweden north of its southernmost tip of Skåne and Finland. The main strategic objective here was to maintain Finnish territorial sovereignty and its ability to resist Soviet overtures, and thus to prevent Soviet advances westward. In spite of its sensitive location, the direct strategic interest for this subregion was rather limited in US planning; it was felt that Finland was in a sense "beyond rescue" after the FCMA Treaty with the Soviet Union in 1948.[22] In the early years of the Cold War, President Truman remarked on the strategic role that Finland had been forced to play in the bipolar game, stating that "now [Soviet] pressure is put on Finland, risking the entire Scandinavian Peninsula."[23] Several years later, the Chief of US Naval Operations explained that the objective of Soviet planning, as he saw it, was to "make Finland into another Latvia, Sweden into another Finland, and Norway into another Sweden."[24]

The prime responsibility and role of officially nonaligned Sweden was to act as a buffer zone, securing its Nordic neighbors both east and west by maintaining a strong military apparatus, which in turn was assisted by a top-secret scheme of military cooperation with NATO. Swedish NATO membership was considered both desirable and necessary in Washington only until the early 1950s. From then on it was merely a desirable scenario, as domestic Swedish realities gradually dawned upon Washington. At that point, the military forces were substantially strengthened, and the complex top-secret Swedish–NATO military contacts established. But membership

---

20   See Skogrand and Tamnes 2001.
21   Honkanen 2002a, pp. 44–45.
22   Ries 1982, Appendix.
23   Quoted in *Vårt Försvar*, 8/98 (my translation from the Swedish text).
24   Tamnes 1991, p. 235.

was no longer an absolute requirement for military cooperation with Sweden, a "precious piece of real estate on the Eurasian rim land" from a Washington horizon during the Cold War, as Dörfer puts it.[25]

2.3 The early years

Much of the scholarly work on security in the Nordic region during the Cold War has been devoted to the critical period of the late 1940s. This was the time when the overall design of European security was in the process of being produced, and the diverse strategic choices of the Nordic countries, composing what would become known as the Nordic balance, were being made – involuntarily for Finland with the Treaty of Friendship and Cooperation imposed upon the country by the Soviet Union in 1948.[26] It was still far from clear how the strategically and politically rather independent-minded Nordic region would fit into the new US strategy for Europe which was gradually being formulated after the end of World War II. While the strategic problems on the Continent were obviously of a more urgent nature (at least up until the late 1970s when the Kola Península gained strategic importance), the future direction of the Nordic region was surrounded by a number of uncertainties.

The Nordic region was in many ways a novel part of the world for the US. Prior to the Cold War, the region had long been located within the British sphere of interest, with Atlanticist Norway seen from London as its logical strategic center. The special relationship between Norway and the UK has been described as "an alliance within the Alliance."[27] Many prominent Norwegians had spent World War II in exile in the United Kingdom, among them the Royal Family, which deepened the ties further between the countries. For some time after the end of the war, and also as a consequence of that war, the North of Europe and in particular its Atlantic areas remained a British, rather than an American area of interest.[28] As the new European system unfolded, the US gradually assumed the leading role in the defense of the Continent, as the British became preoccupied with the imminent collapse of their world-spanning empire.

The unclear division of labor between the two major powers also had consequences in the North of Europe. The lack of American familiarity

---

25 SOU 1994, pp. 105, 108. Quote from Dörfer, 2005, p. 7.
26 See Silva 1999 for a detailed study of this period.
27 Tamnes 1991, p. 37.
28 Thune and Ulriksen 2002, p. 125.

with the Nordic societies and ways of life put a strain on the early days of the bilateral relationship.[29] The Norwegians insisted that both the US and the UK be included in *The Northern European Regional Planning Group* in 1949. In a similar fashion, Denmark and Norway argued in favor of a separate Northern command, and that this should include active participation by the US as well as the UK, rather than the Scandinavian Commander proposed by those two leading allies. The outbreak of the Korean War in 1950 modified the UK–US division of labor by pulling US strategic attention as well as Containment (which now also assumed a more military character) generally in a northern direction.

In the early years of the Cold War, the continued Swedish adherence to a nonaligned and neutral doctrine, and what was seen as a stubborn reluctance to choose sides in the ideological conflict that was quickly dividing Europe into two camps, was a primary concern for the US with regards to the region. The Swedish decision in 1948 to initiate discussions with its Scandinavian neighbors on the creation of a *Scandinavian Defense Union* (SDU) caused a substantial amount of frustration in Washington. While the Americans did not per se object to the idea of a Scandinavian Defense Union, they strongly opposed the Swedish government's ambition to turn this into a neutral and nonaligned union, for which the Swedish architects of the proposal in addition quite unrealistically expected to receive US military equipment. Americans and others perceived the SDU as an attempt to distract and deflect Norway and Denmark from participation in the western defense alliance that was simultaneously being planned.[30]

Among American hardliners – foremost among whom was the Ambassador to Stockholm, H. Freeman Matthews – the Swedish proposal was thus seen as an elaborate plan to sabotage the European security project that the US was in the process of organizing with the European powers under its own auspices. Always inclined to discuss the post-war world in uncompromisingly moral terms, and to make demands of political loyalty from the Swedish government, Matthews found himself regularly clashing with Foreign Minister Östen Undén. The two men could hardly have been more different: the Swedish Foreign Minister, a law professor turned politician, was known for having a soft ideological spot for the Soviet Union (feelings not shared by most of his colleagues in the government nor by the Swedish population).

---

29 Silva 1999. Similar problems would emerge years later in the Baltic region, as Freden recalls, 2006 pp. 252, 263.
30 On the SDU, see for instance Dahl 2002c.

Undén's neutralist views, combined with the Swedish record during World War II of quietly assisting the stronger party (whoever that happened to be at the specific moment) in spite of an official policy of neutrality, made Ambassador Matthews conclude that the Swedes could not be trusted to put up a very strong defense against Soviet pressures, if needed. A number of Swedish military reforms right after the war, channeling government spending from defense to social programs, strengthened this impression.[31] At that point, the Swedish military preparedness could be considered strong only if compared with the Norwegian and Danish defense, both in tatters after the German occupation. Norway, for whom guarantees of military assistance from the West was the number one defense priority, finally opted out of the SDU project, quickly followed by Denmark. Both countries would shortly thereafter become founding members of NATO in April 1949.

That step marked the definite end of the SDU project. But not even the Swedish Government that initiated the project seemed to fully embrace the proposal. The plan, critics argued, was more the result of domestic politics in Sweden, with toughly contested parliamentary elections in 1948, than a sincere effort to restructure and strengthen regional security. The two main political opposition parties, the Liberals and the Conservatives, found the idea of closer ties with the Nordic neighbors very attractive, as did the Swedish military which has traditionally favored regional cooperation.[32] The Non-Socialist opposition wanted a security policy more in tune with American objectives, and nonalignment to be explicitly pro-Western in nature. To them, nonalignment was seen primarily as an instrument to assist Finland, under strong pressure from its belligerent Soviet neighbor. In late 1948 and early 1949, the pro-American forces in Sweden launched a campaign to repair the serious lapse in relations with the US resulting from the collapsed SDU project. Swedish military officers went to great lengths to persuade the US of their country's gradually improved level of preparedness.[33]

The Swedish SDU proposal was thus based on the assumption that the Union would be in a position to purchase arms from the US. The US had, however, absolutely no interest in supplying arms to a nonaligned defense union. In the absence of a commitment to fully participate in the defense of the Western world – that is, membership in NATO – Sweden encountered major difficulties in purchasing the supplies needed even for

31   Silva 1999, 30 ff.
32   Dahl 2002c discusses the views of the Non-Socialist parties towards the SDU.
33   Silva 1999, 275 ff.

her own national defense.³⁴ Referring to the (albeit vague) formulations of the *National Security Council* document (NSC 28) which defined US policy to Scandinavia, Ambassador Matthew's recommendation to Washington was to meet Swedish "isolationism with isolation," and not to agree to the arms deliveries requested by Sweden (in particular air and ground radar) as long as it maintained a nonaligned stance.³⁵ Similar problems emerged during the negotiations for the Marshall Plan, during which Sweden initially did not accept US conditions for participation. In addition, there were political objections in Washington, DC to inviting neutral Sweden as a participant in this project to assist European economic recovery.³⁶

However, bilateral relations made a positive turn in the new decade. In the new statement by the NSC in 1952, NATO membership was abandoned as a requirement for providing assistance to Sweden. At that point, Matthews had been replaced as US ambassador after failing to convince his superiors, and Secretary of State Dean Acheson, of the need to isolate "the disloyal" Swedes.³⁷ With a strengthened military force, Sweden was now in a position, according to the more conciliatory forces at the State Department, to make a substantial contribution not only to its own defense but also to that of its neighbors, most significantly to the two neighboring NATO allies, Denmark and Norway. As a result, negotiations on arms deliveries were concluded, and Sweden could step into the new role as a "silent partner" to NATO, or its "17th member" as the country became known at NATO HQ. It was a position that it would secretly enjoy for the duration of the Cold War (though according to a recent study, this role was gradually reduced during the 1980s).³⁸

The disguised scheme of cooperation with NATO upon which nonaligned Sweden now embarked through bilateral contacts with a number of allies, primarily the UK, the US, Norway, and Denmark, covered a broad range of fields. Among them were intelligence sharing with NATO allies on Soviet activities in the Baltic Sea; the opening of a CIA office at the US Embassy in Stockholm (although there had previously been an OSS office there during World War II); accommodating Swedish air bases and airports to facilitate their use by American B-52 bombers on their way to and from operations in the east; organizing a bilateral exchange program for military officers with the US, and much more. At one point,

---

34 Ibid, pp. 272 ff.
35 Silva 1999, p. 73, NSC 28 (see SOU 1994, Appendix).
36 Ibid, pp. 103 ff.
37 SOU 1994:11, Appendix.
38 According to Dalsjö 2006.

the Swedish Defense Minister even handed the British military a full copy of the Swedish defense plan.[39] Throughout the Cold War, officially nonaligned Sweden also participated in the Western embargo against the Eastern European countries.[40] From a Swedish perspective, these were all measures aimed at ensuring that the country would be in a position to receive support from the West in the event of a Soviet attack.

The US was primarily interested in the support that Sweden could give to its Nordic neighbors in NATO and to regional stability, thereby facilitating US operations eastwards. While the western part of Scandinavia, with the Northern Flank, the western Sea Lanes, and the Baltic Exits, was seen as vital to the US, Sweden itself was considered of relatively minor interest for the US at this early stage of the Cold War. In US planning, Sweden's strategic position resulted from the greater value attached to Norwegian and Danish security. The US thus only accepted nonalignment, and agreed to military support, once Sweden had proved itself capable of making a military contribution to the defense of the entire region.

2.4 "Keep them strong"

Two basic and simple principles guided the American approach to the Nordic countries from an early stage during the Cold War: a US intention to "keep them friendly" so as to maintain them within the Western ideological sphere, and secondly, to "keep them strong" to enable them to survive as free and independent nations.[41] A statement of American policy toward Scandinavia from 1960 outlines the role of the three countries to the US generally:

> The Scandinavian countries are of political interest to the United States for several reasons. First, they are regarded throughout the world as prime examples of Western democracy. Second, there are strong cultural, sentimental and family ties between Scandinavia and the United States. Third, because the Scandinavian countries enjoy considerable prestige in the international community, their support of U.S. policy is valuable in international organizations and for general purposes. Fourth, any Soviet threat to Scandinavian security would create severe apprehension among the other northern European NATO allies who would feel seriously exposed.[42]

39 SOU 1994, pp. 161ff., 291ff.
40 See Karlsson 1992 for an analysis of Swedish trade relations with the Eastern bloc during the early years of the Cold War.
41 This is also the title of the book by Silva 1999; also Tamnes 1991, p. 58.
42 NSC 6006/1 (1960), cited in SOU 1994:11, Appendixes p. 133.

The need to maintain Nordic friendliness resulted in the change of policy toward nonaligned Sweden made explicit in an NSC document in 1952 (although the actual change of policy has been dated to around 1950). Thus, only a few years after Swedish attempts to organize a neutral Scandinavian Defense Union had collapsed, the US no longer required Sweden to join NATO in order to receive assistance. Concluding that such expectations were likely to be fruitless, considering the state of the domestic opinion, and recognizing the recent and rapid buildup of the Swedish military as an asset to the entire region, the National Security Council argued that:

> Although on balance, and primarily because of the advantage to the organization of Scandinavian defense, it would be to our interest to have Sweden in NATO, we must for the predictable future accept as a political fact Sweden's policy of avoiding great power military alliances and calculate accordingly those means and methods best designed to increase Sweden's contribution to Western defense.[43]

In 1962, the Kennedy Administration replaced the two-year old NSC 60006/1 with a 19-page Memorandum specifying the guidelines for US policy and operations toward Sweden.[44] This Memorandum, which was prepared by the Bureau of Northern European Affairs at the State Department instead of by the NSC as with previous documents, and which has Sweden, rather than Scandinavia, as its focus, moves US policy several steps forward when establishing that, although officially nonaligned, Sweden is to be defended by the United States in times of war. This informal and unilateral security guarantee would remain in practice throughout the Cold War, or at least until the first years of the Reagan Administration.[45] Although the NATO allies were apparently not informed of this unilateral US policy decision, officially neutral and nonaligned – and sometimes openly anti-American – Sweden occupied a nonofficial position as a functional, if not actual, ally within NATO, referred to as the "17th member" of the 16-member Alliance. This policy corresponded with the US ambition to ensure that the Nordic countries had the ability to withstand Soviet pressures.

In the Finnish case, US policy departed from the view that apart from encouraging Finland's neighbors to the west to maintain close contact with their strategically and politically exposed friend, nothing should be

---

43 Ibid. and NSC 121 (1952), p. 114 in Appendixes.
44 "Guidelines for Policy and Operations – Sweden", June 1962. In SOU 2002:108, pp. 222 ff.
45 SOU 2002:108, p. 224.

done which could in any way "threaten the delicate balance of Finnish-Soviet relations," and thus, further expose the already vulnerable Finns.[46] A similar document to the one outlining the unilateral policy toward Sweden was presented only a few months later, in January 1963, with regard to Finland. The differences are striking; while the US is prepared to come to nonaligned Sweden's defense, there is no such readiness when it comes to Finland. Instead, the 1963 Memorandum is characterized by a defensive American approach to Finnish security, and by an explicit lack of trust in President Kekkonen.[47]

2.5 From massive retaliation to maritime strategy

Military Containment was implemented through a number of strategic doctrines during the five decades of the bipolar system (1945–1991). George Kennan had early on listed those vital areas where he suggested that the US should focus its strategic interest and "which we cannot permit ... to fall in hands hostile to us." On that list, Scandinavia was integrated into the Atlantic community, but the same perspective was applied to the larger Nordic region.[48] Initially, the US had been unsure of how to incorporate the Nordic region into its defense system, a concern that still prevailed after Norway had entered into NATO.[49] Kennan's listing was primarily due to the strategic vulnerability of Norway, and American fear that the country might be pressured by the Soviet Union to sign a friendship and cooperation treaty similar to that which Finland had been forced to sign.[50]

Kennan's argument was later boiled down to a list of five centers of vital military and industrial power in the world. Apart from the US itself, the areas included Great Britain, Germany and Central Europe, the Soviet Union, and Japan.[51] On this list of what Kennan called the *strongpoints*, neither Scandinavia nor the Nordic region were explicitly included. Nevertheless, a number of strategic roles were assigned to the North during the era of Containment.

---

46 NSC 121, in SOU 1994, p. 116.
47 "Guidelines for Policy and Operations – Finland", January 1963. In SOU 2002:108.
48 Gaddis 1982, p. 30.
49 Zakheim 1998, p. 118.
50 Lundestad 1980, pp. 178 ff.
51 Ibid. Tamnes 1991, p. 21.

However, the absolute predominance of the Central Front in the strategy of massive retaliation by necessity granted Northern Europe a secondary role. Still, the military problems associated with the defense of the flanks preoccupied a small, if distinguished, group of supporters already in the early stages of the Cold War, the most prominent among them, then-SACEUR General Eisenhower. Norwegian historian Rolf Tamnes explains the role of the region in Alliance strategy:

> The strategic rationale behind the Scandinavian alternative [which General Eisenhower advocated] was the significance of the Northern region as a tactical flank area to the Central Front. The flanks could then serve as bridge-heads from which the defense or reconquest of Europe could be initiated ... the General wanted to defend this center by attacking from the flanks.

Thus, the Northern Flank was only of tactical interest with "... the Central Region ... as the indisputable strategic center of the Alliance."[52]

The grand strategy of Containment was thus carried out through a succession of military doctrines. The first of those was the doctrine of *massive retaliation,* in retrospect perhaps most closely identified with the concept of Containment in spite of its rather short duration. This doctrine displayed only a limited interest for the Northern part of Europe. Massive retaliation departed from the idea of a third world war that would follow a single, rapid, and massive nuclear superpower exchange after a Soviet expansionist move on the Central Front. In such a scenario, there was little room for drawn-out warfare in areas outside Central Europe. As Petersen argues, in terms of the amount of attention received, Northern Europe has generally benefited when strategic planners calculated with scenarios of longer, rather than shorter, incidents of bipolar conflict.[53] The result of these military priorities was a strong sense of neglect in the region. Consequently, Denmark and Norway both voiced concerns when NATO discussed the nuclear strategy based on the doctrine of massive retaliation in 1954. In spite of this, the North Atlantic Council approved the new Strategic Concept a few years later.[54]

The general perspective on the Nordic region departed from the idea that military relevance increased with the geographic proximity to the Front, making the Baltic Exits the regional strategic center. As a result of these priorities and as part of the subregion closest to the Central Front, Denmark thus found itself in a prominent strategic position at this time.

---

52 Ibid, p. 67.
53 Petersen 1987, pp. 18 ff.
54 Villaume 1999, p. 36, Honkanen 2002a, p. 50.

Geographically, the small NATO country was sufficiently close to the Central Front to become part of the actual theater in the event of war. In the years prior to German rearmament, which began in 1957, Denmark played a key role as the sole NATO ally located near, and controlling, the Baltic Exits. Prior to the creation of the BALTAP Command at the end of the 1950s, the southern part of Denmark bordering on Schleswig-Holstein had been practically unguarded by the West.[55]

Massive retaliation was replaced by the doctrine of *flexible response* in 1967 in an attempt by NATO to "restore the vitality of Containment." Massive retaliation was at this point considered as too rigid to serve as an effective instrument of deterrence. The role of nuclear forces was reduced in the new doctrine in favor of greater flexibility; the nuclear capacity was seen to have lost some of its deterrent power once also acquired by the Soviet Union. In the North, a considerable gap in conventional power between the two sides (to Soviet advantage) had created a new concern for US strategic planners.[56] On the one hand, the introduction of an element of unpredictability in US strategy, and of the idea that an American response to a Soviet attack could take place anywhere, and take any form and dimension – nuclear or conventional – highlighted the vulnerability of the flanks. Denmark was particularly concerned about the consequences if nuclear deterrence failed, but also a number of European allies objected to the new strategic thinking on the grounds that it made the Continent as a whole more vulnerable.[57] On the other hand, flexible response also raised the threshold for a nuclear attack, which was seen as positive by the two Scandinavian NATO allies, both of whom in the end also gave their support to the new nuclear doctrine in the NAC – "almost by instinct" by Denmark.[58]

In addition, technological developments contributed at this point to reducing the strategic significance attached to geographic location. The military perspective gradually moved north in part as a result of the doctrine of flexible response, but the intensified demand for top-notch intelligence posed by an increasingly high-tech society also played a role. Such demands were especially urgent in the High North where the enemy was right across the border. The assistance that Sweden provided the Alliance, sharing valuable intelligence on the Soviet military activities to

---

55 Petersen 1987, p. 18.
56 Myers, 1989, p. 62, Tamnes 1991, pp. 185 ff., 200.
57 Hillingsø 2004, p. 196.
58 Quote by Faurby 1995, p. 62 in Villaume 1999, p. 40, Honkanen 2002a, p. 50.

the West, was an important factor behind the favorable treatment granted to this neutral and nonaligned country.[59]

The change of perspective in a northern direction was primarily the result of US strategy, and to a lesser extent part of Alliance policy. At SHAPE, military planners maintained their focus on the Central Front, and following that logic, on the Baltic exits. NATO thereby granted Denmark and the area surrounding that country a greater strategic value than was the case at the Pentagon, where the High North was in the process of becoming identified as the most vital of the Nordic subregions at this time.[60]

The 1960s and 70s were in many ways a difficult time for the US. An increased number of out-of-area commitments for the US, foremost among them the long and costly war in Vietnam, were reflected in a less Eurocentric world view in Washington. The combined force of military and political humiliations in the South-Asian jungle as well as in domestic politics, when an American president was forced to resign, had severe consequences for US relations with Europe and for national security generally. Contrary to the military priorities which had guided American national security during the first decades of the Cold War, when the clear objective was strategic superiority, the goals in the 1970s were humbly downsized, and even reached the point where policy-makers and military analysts in the US were forced for the first time to think in terms of future strategic inferiority vis-à-vis the Soviet Union.[61]

This situation, with US superpower leadership in jeopardy, also had a clear impact on American policy toward specific regions; in particular with regard to areas such as the Nordic region, which were geographically remote from the increasingly introverted Washington scene. Discussing US policy toward NATO ally and Soviet neighbor Norway, Ausland points out that:

> ... during the Viet Nam war, US forces in Europe were so decimated that they were not a credible force even on the Central Front. Hence there was little to spare for the Northern Flank. In fact, during this period, the total planned reinforcement for Norway was one fighter squadron ... if additional squadrons had come to Norway, there would have been no preparations for them to fight after they

---

59 For example, NSC 121 (1952), NSC 6006/1 (1960), in SOU 1994, Chapter 4 and Appendixes.
60 SOU 1994, pp. 209, 277.
61 Tamnes 1991, pp. 225 ff.

arrived. That is, there would have been no hard shelters, no ammunition, and no spare parts. Nor would the pilots have familiarized themselves with the Norwegian environment, which would be essential to effective operations.[62]

That the strategic attention of the US was focused elsewhere in this period is illustrated by Henry Kissinger's much-cited question in 1974, "Where in hell is Spitzbergen?"[63]

While the US was torn with domestic problems and debating its role and future as a world power, the Soviet Union was not idly wasting its time. The Soviet Northern fleet had seen a steady increase in size and military strength from the late 1950s onward, passing the Baltic fleet as the core of the Soviet Navy in the early 1980s. This naval buildup launched the traditionally continental Soviet Union onto the global scene as a naval power, challenging US control of the sea and dramatically increasing American strategic vulnerability, with the protective shield previously offered by the oceans removed.[64]

The fast developments on the Kola Península and in the Arctic waters (which reduced the strategic pressure on the Baltic exits) provided the grounds for a revolutionary buildup of US forces in general, and the Navy in particular, in the 1980s. A more aggressive American stance surfaced, particularly evident in the first of Ronald Reagan's two presidencies and characterized by a restored American confidence, US confrontation with the Soviet adversary, and a dramatic arms race. This was the era of the *Maritime Strategy*.[65]

This process reduced the level of tension at the Central Front, but the arms race continued, and even intensified, on the Northern Flank.[66] The turn of strategic focus, which resulted from this new chapter in superpower relations, also affected the Western strategy vis-à-vis the Nordic region, where the Continental perspective centered on Denmark thus lost prominence to the High North in the later half of the Cold War. The Northern Flank now became the Northern *Front*.[67]

As we have seen, military Containment was implemented through a range of strategic instruments in the Nordic region during the Cold War. A number of shifts in strategic attention, interest, and focus, occurred

62 Ausland 1986, pp. 120 and 133.
63 Cited in Tamnes 1991, p. 241.
64 Myers 1989, pp. 7 ff.
65 Tamnes 1991, pp. 271 ff.
66 Ibid, pp. 278 ff.
67 Thune and Ulriksen 2002, p. 126.

over the years in Washington and Brussels with regard to the region as a whole as well as its subregions. From the position as a tactical flank serving the Central Front in the early 1950s, the region (and its northern parts in particular) gained strategic prominence – and in some ways increased vulnerability – with the strategy of flexible response. A new, parallel role as a strategic flank emerged in the late 1970s, and for parts of the region, as a strategic front in the 1980s.[68]

Generally, speaking, the Nordic region thus had more success in attracting the strategic attention of the US bilaterally than through NATO. On the other hand, such bilateral American interest was always the result of a troublesome military presence in the area from the Soviet Union, which was hardly for the region's common good. The Nordic region, Myers notes, was not a region where a third world war would have been won; but it was one where it could have been lost.[69]

---

68 Ibid, p. 296.
69 Myers 1989, p. 64.

3. The Nordic Region in Ideological Containment

3.1 Solid democracies in the West

Following the reasoning of George Kennan, who tended to view the relationship with the Soviet Union from a political rather than a military perspective, an ideological strategy was needed parallel to the military one in order to provide a complete and successful Containment strategy. Consequently, Containment originally dealt with the threat that was emanating from Moscow in primarily political or ideological terms.[70] With the pattern of amity and enmity – in Buzan terminology – such an ideological dimension is added to the geopolitical features of the international system, the global distribution of power discussed on previous pages.[71] Norwegian historian Rolf Tamnes uses a similar division in his detailed analysis of US policy on the Northern Flank.[72] Taken together, these two features cover a broad spectrum of superpower relations.

The half-century of polarized ideological conflict and international tension that characterized the bipolar world during the Cold War represented, historically speaking, a unique institutionalization of enmity. Bipolarity affected everyone and everybody in the international system; a clear majority of the world's nations found themselves siding with one or the other of the superpowers, voluntarily or as a result of the exercise of some form of force.

70 Gaddis 1982, for example pp. 25 ff.
71 Buzan 1991, pp. 189 ff.
72 See Tamnes 1991.

This was true also in the Nordic region, which throughout the Cold War years was characterized by the existence of a military-strategic – but not ideological – "Nordic balance" between East and West. From an ideological perspective, the Nordic area constituted one, single region, rather than the number of subregions that divided the region from a strategic perspective.

While the region, as we have seen, presented a complex picture in the realm of security policy, with a broad range of (official) doctrines, the similarities in policies were often striking beyond the strategic level. This group of Northern nations formed a cohesive entity of peaceful and stable democracies with advanced social welfare systems, although with some national discrepancies and a variety of historical experiences For an outsider, the three Scandinavian countries in particular came across as created from the same mold, with similar cultural and linguistic identities. The almost identical set of values that united all five Nordic countries, and which was translated into similar domestic policies, was also reflected in their international image as a region of remarkable domestic and cultural cohesion.

Regardless of a certain Nordic attraction for Socialist-inspired and state-controlled welfare models, it was equally obvious that all countries belonged in the Western camp as open, free, and exceptionally solid democracies. This, in combination with the traditional Nordic fondness for a neutral stance, and the reluctance to openly side with the US in world affairs, puzzled many outsiders. Swedish and Finnish neutrality could to a large extent (but not exclusively) be derived from geopolitical causes, but the inclination to go for the neutral option and to keep a certain distance from the US also had distinct ideological aspects, primarily in the Swedish, but also in the Norwegian and Danish cases.

3.2   Neutrality and NATO conditions

From the perspective of (official) security doctrines, the pattern that emerged among the five Nordic countries was thus one of division rather than cohesion; between themselves the five countries managed to present a grand total of three, or even four (if separating Swedish and Finnish nonalignment, as should be done), doctrines. In the eastern part of the region, Finland had little say in its choice of security doctrine, and also in other ways had to take Soviet reactions and concerns into constant consideration. The FCMA Treaty of 1948 with the Soviet Union placed Finland in exceptionally difficult circumstances, with the Finns having to use great caution in their dealings with their giant neighbor to the east. But while Finland had been a participant in World War II, and emerged with a neutralist security policy as a result of Soviet pressures, Swedish nonalignment resulted from an independent and sovereign decision. Concern for Finland, which had formed the eastern province of Sweden until 1809, also played a crucial role in the official justification of Swedish nonalignment (the so-called "Finnish argument").[73]

Although nonalignment has been the official doctrine of only two Nordic countries since World War II, neutrality had historically been the first choice for the entire region prior to that war. The neutralist tradition is a regional trademark: a general ambition to remain outside of conflict that has long united the actors of the region in recent historic times.

In the Finnish case, this ambition has not been as successful as it has for its neighbors. While Finland had to fight for its independence repeatedly in the course of the 20th century, the German occupation of Denmark and Norway in 1940 marked a brutal interruption of their neutral foreign policies, and paved the way for their post-war NATO membership jointly with Iceland (which hosted an American military presence on the island during World War II and afterwards, but holds no military forces of its own). Only Sweden managed to maintain a neutral doctrine (officially) throughout World War II. But although the Swedish position outside of the war is often credited to the neutral policy, in reality it was more the result of skillful diplomatic maneuvering.[74]

Nowhere has the Nordic pacifist, and in some ways isolationist, tendency been more visible than in Sweden. The voluntary Swedish position in between the two blocs – with NATO to the West, and a friendship and cooperation pact imposed upon Finland by the Soviet Union to the East – was in many ways characteristic of a general Nordic tendency to seek compromises and consensus. Over the years, neutrality had become a vital part of the national identity, and the idea that neutrality had saved Sweden from war since Napoleonic times is still a cherished national myth. The national tendency to opt for the "golden" middle way was also allowed to influence the country's official security policy throughout the entire Cold War (and thereafter).[75] Only very few had knowledge of the secret scheme of cooperation with NATO and the close military contacts with the West that were maintained by the Swedish government and the military leader-

---

73 On the "Finnish" argument, see Dahl 2002c, pp. 220 ff., and Kronvall 2003.
74 For a study of Sweden during World War II, see Carlgren 1977.
75 Nilsson (Dahl) 1991a.

ship throughout the Cold War, parallel with a strict official adherence to the "Third Way."

As we have seen, the traditional neutralist inclinations of the region surfaced again after World War II. The Swedish proposal in 1948 for a Scandinavian Defense Union, while preparations for an Atlantic defense organization were under way, came to a definite end when Sweden insisted that the pact be based on a neutral security doctrine (but nevertheless expected it to receive American arms deliveries).[76] With Finland unable to participate because of Soviet pressure on this small Nordic neighbor, and with Iceland having already turned to the United States for its military assistance, the negotiations were limited to the Scandinavian, rather than the Nordic group of countries. In reality, only Sweden and Denmark took the option of a Scandinavian defense alliance into serious consideration. Although Norway did engage in the defense negotiations, the Atlanticist country never saw "Norden" as a viable alternative to the transatlantic link, in part because of the historical animosity with Sweden which Norway still harbored more than 40 years after the dissolution of the Swedish–Norwegian Union. This sentiment was reinforced during World War II when Nazi troops and reinforcements were allowed to pass through formally neutral Sweden on their way to occupied Norway.[77]

Swedish efforts to establish an alternative defense pact, although armed by the West, were not appreciated by the US, which looked upon such independent neutralist policies with great suspicion.[78] But also the two Scandinavian countries that in the end joined the Atlantic Alliance as charter members (with Iceland as a third Nordic country in NATO) possessed an independent political streak that had a tendency to complicate life for NATO in general and the Americans in particular. Many of the issues discussed may have been military in nature – such as the conditions of membership in NATO or opposition to nuclear weapons – but the background for the positions pursued by the Scandinavians was often purely political.

The conditions imposed by the Scandinavian countries for their membership in NATO were made in response to a combination of domestic considerations and the political pressure exerted at this time by the Soviet Union. Intelligence sources claimed to have evidence that Denmark was next in line for a Communist coup after the one in Prague in February

---

76 For an analysis of the Scandinavian Defense Union from the perspective of domestic Swedish politics, see Dahl 2002c, pp. 205 ff. The former Foreign Minister of Denmark, Uffe Elleman-Jensen, describes the proposal as Danish (2004, p. 55).
77 Thune and Ulriksen 2002, p. 125.
78 See for instance NSC 28/1 (1948) in SOU 1994:11, Appendix p. 26.

1948; Norway, on the other hand, could soon expect a Soviet "offer" of a friendship pact similar to the one presented to Finland.[79] The Norwegian government immediately turned to Great Britain for help; a move which a year later contributed to the establishment of the Atlantic Alliance. The Danes were in a more vulnerable military situation than either the Norwegians or the Swedes – according to military estimates, Denmark could not only be occupied in the course of a single night, but in addition, this could be done without the Soviet Union having to fear much of an American reaction.[80] According to intelligence sources, of all the European countries that remained outside Soviet control, small Denmark was the one least likely to provoke a full-scale war between the superpowers if it were occupied.

During the negotiations, Norway and Denmark presented a number of unilateral conditions when joining the Alliance. The Scandinavian conditions concerned two areas: foreign troops, which Norway and Denmark refused to have stationed on their territory in peacetime, and nuclear weapons. The one exception was the two American bases on Greenland, of which Thule was the more important, but then there had already been American troops stationed in Greenland during World War II. Denmark was in no position to defend the huge territory of Greenland without US assistance – in fact, Greenland was one of main reasons for Denmark joining the Atlantic Alliance. In addition, from the 1950s on, the two Scandinavian NATO allies would not allow military exercises on the territory of Northern Finnmark, bordering the Soviet Union, or on the Danish island of Bornholm in the Baltic Sea, nor naval or air-force exercises east of Bornholm.

With no military forces of its own but with a geopolitically vital location in the Atlantic Sea midway between the continents, Iceland reluctantly agreed to host a foreign presence, as long as this was confined to the area occupied by the American base.[81] But the American base at Keflavik was twice threatened with closure, in 1956 and 1973, after popular objections to the US presence on the island (even though the American soldiers were allowed only very limited access to Icelandic territory outside the base).[82]

---

79   Ellemann-Jensen, 2004 p. 52.
80   Ibid, p. 54, Hillingsø 2004, p. 25.
81   Petersen 1987, pp. 23ff, Petersen 1990, pp. 92–92.
82   Jonsson 1989 offers a comprehensive study of Iceland and NATO, with particular emphasis on the Keflavik base. Also Ries 1982, p. 53.

3.3 Deterrence and détente

Having successfully negotiated a number of conditions in their "à la carte" membership, the Scandinavian NATO allies quickly became known as strong advocates for a more nuanced approach to fighting the enemy than sole reliance on military deterrence. They repeatedly tried to find ways to "soften" the doctrine of massive retaliation, and they welcomed the new doctrine of flexible response, with its higher nuclear threshold.[83] The Harmel Report, which established the twin purposes of deterrence and détente by adding confidence-building measures to the tasks performed by the Alliance, was based on a Scandinavian draft, and the two Scandinavian allies were enthusiastic supporters of this broader agenda.[84] The adoption of the Harmel Report by the NATO Council in December 1967 was seen as a major victory for Denmark and Norway, and the conciliatory attitude they represented, by adding confidence-building measures to the agenda. By embarking on its dual task, NATO had now become more "Nordic."

Nevertheless, the Nordic countries in and outside the Alliance found themselves increasingly in political confrontation with the NATO agenda in the 1970s and 80s. A number of proposals were introduced for nuclear-free zones of varying geographic extension and location.[85] The idea of a nuclear-free zone in the Nordic region had first appeared at a Stockholm peace conference in 1954. A Finnish proposal on the subject was launched by President Kekkonen in 1963, outlining a nuclear-free zone in the Nordic region and Baltic Sea. Two decades later the idea was again raised in a speech in October 1980 by the Norwegian ambassador and ex-minister Jens Evensen. The Palme Commission, presided over by the Swedish Prime Minister, also proposed a 150-kilometer wide nuclear-free, low-tension zone surrounding the Iron Curtain.

The Danish Social Democrats had previously been skeptical of any arrangement that didn't also include Soviet territory, but warmed to the idea in the 1980s, when the concept of a nuclear-free zone was introduced as a key part of their campaign against nuclear weapons in Denmark and the rest of Europe.[86] These proposals, made without any requests for a Soviet quid pro quo, were seen by the Nordic countries themselves as confidence-building measures and as important contributions to the strengthening of East–West détente.[87] The US and NATO saw things quite differ-

---

83 Villaume 1999, pp. 39–40.
84 Honkanen 2002a, p. 51, Villaume 1999, p. 38.
85 See Dörfer 1991, pp. 128 pp. for a thorough analysis of the free zone debate.
86 Villaume 1999, p. 45.
87 See for instance Brundtland 1985, p. 210, Zakheim 1998, p. 122, Villaume 1999, p. 45.

ently; as seriously undermining NATO strategy and as a hostile attack on Western democracy. Secretary of State Alexander Haig made this bluntly clear to his Norwegian counterpart at a meeting in August 1981, from which Foreign Minister Knut Frydenlund emerged in a state of shock after the confrontation with the American.[88] President Reagan explained that he considered the Nordic campaign for a nuclear-free zone slightly ironic at a time when "unidentified" submarines were intruding into Swedish territory.[89] The Nordic free zone disappeared from the political agenda with the arrival of the Conservative Willoch and Schlüter governments in Norway and Denmark respectively.[90]

The stationing of Cruise and Pershing missiles in the heart of the European continent in response to Russian SS-20s, provoked massdemonstrations against US policy in many parts of Europe. At the NATO Council meeting in December 1979, Denmark proposed a six-month postponement or freezing of the dual-track decision to deploy Cruise and Pershing II missiles in Western Europe, while in the meantime an offer was to be made to the Soviets for a negotiated INF-settlement, and for disarmament talks to be held with Moscow. Denmark finally accepted the dual-track strategy, after its own proposal for negotiations with the Soviet Union was soundly rejected by the other NATO allies.[91] A similar proposal – also unsuccessful – had already been made in 1957, when Denmark and Norway proposed postponing the NATO deployment of medium-range nuclear missiles in Western Europe until after negotiations with the Soviet Union.[92]

3.4 Footnotes

Danish formal objections to the political decisions made by the Alliance created the new category of "footnote member" in the 1980s, as remarks explaining the minority position of the Danish government with regard to security issues in the Folketing were regularly filed with the joint communiqués and decisions. Becoming referred to as "footnotes," such remarks were added to decisions dealing with nuclear issues and missile defense, such as the financing and deployment of the INF, the Reagan

---

88 Dörfer 1991, p. 137.
89 Ibid, p. 140.
90 Ibid, p. 135. Tamnes gives a detailed discussion of this period in 1997, chapter 4.
91 Villaume 1999, p. 42–43. For a detailed discussion of the domestic Danish debate and security policy process, see Ellemann-Jensen 2004, pp. 96 ff.
92 Villaume 1999, p. 36.

SDI-initiative, as well as contributions to NATO's infrastructure program. At this time, Denmark also turned down an invitation to participate in the technological research for the SDI, to the obvious irritation of their US colleagues.

Although the period is generally seen as having started in 1982, when "the alternative majority" took control of the security agenda in the Folketing, the first Danish footnote was filed on June 10, 1983, at the meeting of NATO foreign ministers in Brussels. The first "footnote" – which in reality was a comment added to the protocol – demonstrated the complex political situation in which Denmark found itself at this time:

> The Danish Minister of Foreign Affairs repeated Danish Government support for the Double-track decision but at the same time he presented to his colleagues the motion passed by the Folketing on May 26.[93]

The parliamentary motion introduced by the "alternative majority" consisted of a four-point program with proposals such as an extension of the INF negotiations, a freezing of middle-range weapons, and inclusion of French and British nuclear arsenals in the INF and Start negotiations (in exact accordance with the Soviet positions).[94] If implemented, the demands made by the Folketing majority would have seriously undermined the US position in the ongoing negotiations with the Soviet Union, as then-US Secretary of State George Schultz made clear to his Danish colleague.[95]

On that occasion and later, then-Foreign Minister Uffe Ellemann-Jensen had to explain to his NATO colleagues that although he himself, and the Non-Socialist government he represented, fully supported the political course set by the Alliance, the security policy agenda was controlled by an "alternative majority" of parties and parliamentarians critical of US and NATO policy in general, and the Dual-Track Decision in particular.[96]

By the end of the 1970s, the Social Democrats, then in government, had already encountered mounting domestic criticism to the nuclear arms race and Danish NATO policy from the political left, with strong support by the peace movements and large parts of the press. As they were replaced by a new coalition of Conservative and Liberal parties, the Social Democrats decided to join forces with the parties further to the left and

---

93   Ellemann-Jensen, 2004, p. 142.
94   Ibid, p. 137–139.
95   Villaume 1999, p. 67.
96   Ellemann-Jensen, 2004, p. 142 ff.

the Social Liberal Party. This period from 1982 to 1988 has been described as one of constant strife and confrontation, with the "alternative majority" composed of parties to the left of the center in a position to dictate the security policy agenda. As Ellemann-Jensen eloquently explains in his book *Fodfejl*, this policy was performed with "the acute discomfort" of the Conservative–Liberal government.[97] Denmark's relationship with NATO became characterized by a curious mixture of association and dissociation, and gave the country the image of a "semi-aligned" member of the Alliance. To the other NATO allies, the Danish footnotes represented a severe break with the basic principles of solidarity and loyalty to the Washington Treaty.

In May 1987, as the battle on the Dual-Track decision was coming to an end, Ellemann-Jensen quite simply announced that he refused to continue the humiliating exercise of placing any more footnotes at the end of the NATO documents.[98] The footnote period came to a definite end in 1988 with the election of a new government, after yet another disruptive debate on security – this time the question of whether visiting naval vessels should be notified of the Danish nuclear ban on its territory. Such a policy would have stopped any Danish participation in NATO naval exercises, and jeopardize the delivery of vital reinforcements in times of war. This was pointed out by the US government, which also made it perfectly clear that such a step would have severe consequences for the bilateral defense cooperation and the defense commitments at the core of NATO's Article Five.[99]

Interpreting the vessel controversy as a final, and unacceptable, blow to Denmark's credibility and ability to function as a full member in NATO, Prime Minister Poul Schlüter decided to call parliamentary elections.[100] The elections resulted in the effective dissolution of the "alternative majority" with the small, but central, Social Liberal Party changing sides and joining the coalition government. But as the former Foreign Minister notes, the footnote period also came to an end because the world had changed: the signing of the INF Treaty in December 1987 removed the contentious Double Track issue from the bipolar agenda, and signaled the arrival of détente.[101]

---

97 Petersen 1987, p. 34.
98 Villaume 1999, p. 46, Ellemann-Jensen 2004, p. 234.
99 Ellemann-Jensen, 2004, pp. 241 ff., 251–253.
100 Villaume 1999, pp. 46 ff., Ellemann-Jensen, 2004, pp. 241 ff.
101 Ellemann-Jensen 2004, p. 262.

The six years of "semi-aligned" policy severely damaged every aspect of Denmark's cooperation in NATO. For years afterwards, those representing the country noticed its impact. At meetings at the military level, Danish military officers, with no influence on the policy process, got a chilly reception from their NATO colleagues.[102] In 1990, two years after the footnote era was closed, the military officer responsible for bilateral contacts with NATO quickly came to realize how deep the sentiments of suspicion and mistrust of Danish policy still ran at NATO.[103] The footnote period was, Ellemann-Jensen states, a dark time in the country's history, when Denmark "betrayed its friends and allied partners in NATO," and when the Danish standing in NATO was seriously damaged for years to come. [104]

His American colleague at the time, Secretary of State George Schultz, made his views clear during an official visit on board the training ship "Danmark" in 1985, bluntly stating to Ellemann-Jensen that if all NATO allies behaved like Denmark, there would be no Alliance. And, he added, Europe should not expect the United States to come to its rescue a third time, if the countries on the Continent pursued policies as destructive as Denmark's, which consistently undermined the credibility and strategy of the United States.[105]

Another area of discontent with Denmark, but also with the Norwegian NATO ally, was the size of their defense budgets. Danish defense spending was kept well below NATO recommendations, and regularly led to accusations of freeloading.[106] The Danish contribution at the bottom of the ranking was seen as yet another sign of a lack of solidarity, and at one point provoked the US Secretary of State to write letters of complaint to his Danish colleague, in which he protested against the government proposal for a "zero-solution" in the upcoming defense agreement.[107] Critics warned of a trend of "Denmarkization", if other allies were to follow the Danish example.[108] When NATO took a collective decision to increase defense spending by an annual 3 percent in 1978, Denmark made a formal reservation – and consistently kept its own level of spending at a lower level.[109]

---

102 Hillingsø 2004, p. 64 ff.
103 Hillingsø, 2004, p. 7 (foreword by Karsten Møller).
104 Ellemann-Jensen 2004, 7 ff.
105 Ibid, pp. 202 ff.
106 Petersen 1990, p. 92.
107 Villaume 1999, p. 43.
108 Ibid, p. 43.
109 Ibid, p. 33; Honkanen 2002a, p. 56.

Meanwhile, Norway was criticized for spending too much on personnel and not enough on procurement.[110] Norway and Denmark both "failed to take their NATO contributions seriously enough," as seen from Washington.[111] There were other complaints as well: an American document from 1961, discussing the fact that Norwegian ships had been discovered on their way to blockaded Cuba, and criticizing Norway for not supporting the US during the Berlin crisis, describes Norway as "a cool member" of NATO.[112] Although Norway as a result of its geography and history was actually one of the most Western-oriented countries in NATO, the activist bridge-building policy pursued by the country was characterized as an example of "diluted Atlanticism."[113]

3.5 "Keep them friendly"

The five Nordic countries share a long history of relying on compromise and consensus in their decision-making processes. In security policy, this tendency was most pronounced in the Swedish and Danish cases (although nonaligned, Finland had no say in its choice of security doctrine because of the proximity to the Soviet Union). Four out of five Nordic countries – Finland being an exception because of its strategically and politically delicate situation – in various ways complicated the US Containment policy by their reluctance to fully and officially join the ideological struggle. The domestic and historic roots of this reluctance were acknowledged in Washington, DC, but the general Nordic attitude nevertheless created the impression of a less than wholehearted commitment to the ideological struggle, which was at the core of the Containment strategy.

Officially neutral and nonaligned Sweden provided the most obvious obstacle for American efforts to ideologically contain the Soviet Union. Underneath the blatantly anti-American outbursts and the Swedish policy of a "Third Way" between what were described in rhetoric as two equally decadent superpowers, a more cooperative attitude to transatlantic relations could be found, with extensive cooperation with the US and other NATO countries.[114] The elaborate, top-secret system of double doctrines was known to only a handful of Swedes in government and the military,

---

110 Honkanen 2002a, p. 56.
111 Moores 2002, p. 52.
112 Tamnes 1991, p. 219.
113 Ibid.
114 Nilsson (Dahl) 1991a.

but US awareness of the scheme facilitated relations in times of diplomatic turmoil. The three NATO allies created their share of trouble for the US as well, by refusing to allow foreign troops and nuclear weapons on their soil in the Danish and Norwegian cases, and repeatedly threatening to close the Keflavik base in the Icelandic case. All three had political difficulties adjusting to the requirements placed upon them as Western countries by the strategy of Containment at the ideological level.

In spite of the problems caused by the independent-minded Nordic countries from an ideological perspective, US policy was to downplay the differences in an effort not to further alienate the countries of the strategically significant region next door to the Soviet Union.

One important instrument of the policy to "keep them friendly" was the extension of the Marshall Plan to all Nordic countries, with the exception of Finland, which declined the offer in order not to antagonize its powerful Soviet neighbor. This policy also included Sweden, which, while insisting that its neutrality not be infringed, received $347 million (only slightly less than Norway and Denmark) in assistance, although it was never a participant in World War II. The agreement was preceded by difficult negotiations. In an effort to avoid a situation of political and financial dependency on American goodwill, Norway and Sweden made a joint proposal for a different organization and distribution of the American assistance.[115] In spite of such difficulties Sweden in the end became both a recipient of Marshall Aid as well as a nonaligned participant of the Western economic embargo against the Eastern European countries.

NATO member Denmark, however, maintained a rather skeptical view of the trade embargo. Denmark considered the embargo as a form of economic warfare and, although participating in the COCOM, was the least cooperative of all NATO countries in the trade embargo, according to US and British diplomats.[116] In practice, nonaligned Sweden thus turned out to be a greater supporter of the trade embargo against the Eastern Bloc in practical terms than NATO-ally Denmark.

As a result of Sweden's participation in the Marshall Plan, Swedish import of key supplies for industry was facilitated, while exports to the other 15 recipient countries increased significantly. Perhaps most importantly, the country's position within the emerging Western bloc as a free and democratic nation was ensured. Parallel to this, attempts to isolate the Swedish Communists (who had faced a substantial election defeat in the

---

115 Karlsson1992, 156ff.
116 Villaume 1999, p. 36–37.

ideologically heated election of 1948) were at times further accelerated by the Social Democratic government.

The offer of financial assistance to a country which had not taken part in the defense of the free world during World War II, and whose need of economic support might have appeared as relatively small compared to the other participating countries (but which nevertheless went through some financial hard times after the war), could be interpreted as an act of US economic and political generosity. But in particular, it indicated American awareness of the delicate situation in which the Nordic countries as a region found themselves, and also of the important role of that region within the grand strategy of Containment.

3.6 Moral superpowers in the North

In addition to the neutralist stance of the Nordic countries, the moralistic approach with which they often approached the surrounding world in the Cold War period also severely complicated relations with the US. Although the US itself has historically used moral as a foreign policy instrument (as was also the case during the Cold War), the Nordic perspective, with a distinct anti-American tilt and explicit opposition and criticism of US policy, was the cause of much frustration. In the Swedish case, the perceived value of the neutral and nonaligned policy, which was presented to the outside world as a model of a "Third Way" between East and West, inspired one prominent representative from the dominant Social Democrats, then-Undersecretary of State Pierre Schori, to rather immodestly describe his own country as the world's "moral superpower."[117] In spite of his open anti-Americanism and declared unwillingness to even visit the US in the 1980s, Schori would later reside in NYC as the Swedish ambassador to the UN.

The activist engagement for revolutionary causes in the Third World departed from the ideological perspective of the Social Democratic government, which saw Sweden as politically located between the two equally decadent, brutal, and immoral – as they saw it – superpowers. In the Third World, the Swedish government acted as a provider of development aid and ideological and financial support to radical movements and regimes, and, less successfully, as a mediator of regional conflicts and an initiator of disarmament initiatives. The latter role occasionally clashed with the

---

117 The phrase was used in a more ironic sense in the title of a book: see Nilsson (Dahl), 1991a.

simultaneous but secret efforts to export Swedish arms; on one occasion, Olof Palme is said to have crossed the street from a disarmament meeting to pursue a secret arms deal in India.

Such activist policies were, however, pursued by all Nordic countries – although Finland carefully avoided a high-profile policy and getting drawn into issues that might raise any questions from Moscow. The activist position of Finland during the Cold War could, Ries argues, be better described as "realpolitik activism," such as the promotion of the CSCE-process starting in 1975.[118] The Nordic countries usually kept defense policy, security policy and foreign policy strictly separated, with heavy compartmentalization of the issues and forums used for the different policies; the UN for foreign policy, NATO for security policy, etc.[119] Of the Nordic neighbors, NATO-ally Norway provided Sweden with the toughest competition for the title of moral superpower, exposing a very ambitious activist agenda of its own.

Similar to Sweden, Norway maintained a high-profile activist policy during the Cold War (and after), and, like Sweden, combined a legalistic approach with an ideological – or idealistic – perspective on world affairs. Norway's opposition to the Vietnam War never reached the Swedish dimension, but the Nordic NATO-ally had provided humanitarian aid to Vietnam in 1972, while the war was still on, as well as to Communist movements at war with NATO-member Portugal in Angola, Mozambique and Cap Verde.[120] In comparison, Danish criticism of US warfare was voiced only very late, and was much more "muted" than the opposition coming from nonaligned Sweden.[121] In the 1980s, Norway turned its idealistic focus to Nicaragua (as did Sweden), and made the Sandinista-run country one of the main recipients of Norwegian support, in sharp contrast to US policy in the region.[122] The independent line in opposition to US policy pursued by Norway (and several other allies) primarily in the Third World, even using NATO as an arena for such criticism, demonstrates the democratic nature of the Alliance as well as the limited control exercised by the US over its partners.[123]

Although foreign policy was usually pursued in other arenas, there were also signs of Scandinavian activism inside NATO. Both Norway and

118 Ries 2002, p. 74f.
119 Holm 2002 p. 87, and Thune and Ulriksen 2002, p. 130.
120 Thune and Ulriksen 2002, p. 130.
121 Holm 2002, p. 88.
122 Thune and Ulriksen 2002, pp. 127ff.
123 This argument is further developed with case studies in Dahl and Hillmer, 2002a.

Denmark actively opposed the 1952 enlargement of NATO with Turkey and Greece on (mainly) political grounds, arguing that neither country met NATO requirements for democracy. While Denmark maintained its opposition (arguing also on strategic grounds against the enlargement, which it saw as a possible provocation to the Soviet Union), Norway decided to drop its opposition prior to the NATO meeting in Ottawa in September 1951. Many years later, both countries again, and on similar grounds, voiced opposition to NATO's enlargement plans to General Franco's Spain.[124]

Opposition to the US, and in particular to the war in Vietnam and US involvement in Central America a decade later, constituted a central part of the moralist-activist rhetoric of officially neutral Sweden. Sweden was the first country in the West to open diplomatic relations with North Vietnam in January 1969. Prime Minister Olof Palme made a strong anti-American point when he appeared next to the North Vietnamese ambassador to Moscow in a candle-lit demonstration against US policy in Stockholm. In late 1972, Palme again infuriated the US with a provocative statement comparing US bombings in Vietnam with Nazi atrocities in the German concentration camps. Ambassador Leif Leifland, who was stationed in Washington at the time of the war, recalls in his memoirs how the American Administration saw the Palme government as "... a bitter, uninformed, and increasingly loud opponent" who paved the way for an international wave of criticism against US policy and went to the top of the Nixon Administration's blacklist. The US also reacted against Sweden's role as a safe haven for American soldiers deserting the Vietnam War.[125]

Although accompanied by similar programs in the other Nordic countries, the vehement criticism expressed by then-Prime Minister Olof Palme was seen as particularly upsetting to Washington, voiced as it was by a country, which had not itself participated in the defense of Europe against Nazism during World War II. On the contrary, German troops passing through Swedish territory on their way to and from occupied Norway was only one example of the pragmatic position assumed by the neutral neighbor during the war, although perhaps the most graphic one. Swedish neutrality had proved a very flexible tool as, toward the end of the war, assistance shifted instead to the Allied side.

---

124 Smith 2000, p. 140, Honkanen 2002, p. 46 ff.
125 On Sweden and the Vietnam War, Leifland 1997. (Citation on pp. 15 ff.)

The consequences of Palme's anti-American outbursts during the Vietnam War were harsh: the US withdrew its ambassador to Stockholm and refused to admit the new Swedish ambassador to Washington to take up his post. The US–Swedish conflict lasted well into the 1980s when relations finally started to normalize. Prime Minister Ingvar Carlsson was greeted at the White House in 1987 on the first official visit by a Swedish premier since the 1950s. Olof Palme had also entertained hopes of an official invitation to the White House, an expectation that the Americans however considered completely unrealistic after his long career as a US detractor. But the long row between the countries was not just a matter of Social Democratic opposition to US policy in Vietnam. An NSC document from the very early stages of the Cold War discusses the problems produced by Sweden in the ideological struggle: it was, at that point, the American ambition "to make perfectly clear to Sweden our dissatisfaction with its apparent failure to discriminate in its own mind and its future planning between the West and the Soviet Union."[126]

This early US position would be modified a few years later in a subsequent policy statement by the National Security Council, in which Swedish neutrality was accepted as a political reality. Attempts to make NATO membership a precondition for US arms deliveries were abandoned as Sweden was making a sincere effort to establish a strong national defense (thereby strengthening the military preparedness of the entire region and enabling Swedish support to the weak Nordic NATO allies).[127] Nevertheless, and in spite of what would become a close, though secret, military partnership, the 1948 declaration was to a large extent reflective of the US view generally to the Swedish official attitude to the ideological division, which defined the Cold War. The very existence of this tacit inclusion of Sweden in NATO planning, and the military assistance provided to the nonaligned country (to which Sweden reciprocated by performing intelligence missions on behalf of NATO and the US, providing landing strips built to accommodate the heavy US bombers, and at one point even sharing top-secret military plans with Britain), made the temperamental outbursts from Stockholm even harder to stomach in Washington, DC.

---

126 NSC 28/1, in SOU 1994:11, Appendix, p. 26.
127 For a detailed analysis of Swedish–US relations from 1948 to 1952, see Silva 1999.

3.7 Innocent Nordic countries

In the US, the moralist rhetoric and policy were seen as evidence of a general Nordic innocence combined with successful Soviet manipulation. From an American perspective, the Nordic countries appeared in general to be much too positively inclined toward the Soviet Union, much too ready to consider Soviet proposals at face value, and as a result were bound to be the victims of Communist manipulation. In the Swedish case, this innocence was somewhat tempered by the discovery of a Soviet submarine – the Whiskey U137 – stuck on top of an island in the southern archipelago in the fall of 1981. To many, this confirmed that the Soviets indeed saw Sweden as semi-NATO territory that the submarine crew had been on assignment to patrol. The incident was the starting point of years of intense Swedish submarine watching.

There has been widespread speculation that the intense Swedish criticism of the US from the mid-1960s on was in reality part of an elaborate plan to appease the Soviets, who turned out to have excellent information about the extensive contacts that the Swedish military maintained with the Pentagon and a number of NATO countries. According to a Swedish historian who has studied the Soviet archives, Moscow was well aware of this cooperation, and as a result considered NATO's eastern border to run in the Baltic Sea, not west of the Swedish border. [128] The anti-American rhetoric would thus have been an attempt to balance the (correct) Soviet impression of Swedish policy as anything but neutral or nonaligned under its rhetorical surface, but actually engaged in an elaborate scheme of cooperation with NATO and the US.

The strong leftist presence in Nordic politics, with a seemingly endless succession of Labor and Socialist/Social Democratic governments, undoubtedly added yet another complication to the relationship. A particular source of irritation among Americans was the tendency among Nordic Socialists and Social Democrats not only to voice criticism of the US, but to export their views and welfare models abroad to their European brothers in the Scandilux group and the Socialist International, as well as to the countries aided by extensive programs of development assistance in the Third World.[129] But although these parties overtly challenged US policy, thereby disturbing the impact of its Cold War struggle, the US also saw them as easy to do business with at a practical level, and even seemed to have favored Socialist parties with long experience of government and

---

[128] See Petersson 1994, pp. 39 ff.
[129] See Dahl (Nilsson) 1991a, Dahl (Nilsson) 1991b.

good records in fighting local Communism over openly pro-American non-Socialists, who in turn found this preference puzzling.[130]

Nevertheless, the arrival of non-Socialist parties in government often resulted in more cordial relations, for example when the Conservative government in Norway won the election in 1981, or when the paralyzing influence of the Left on security policy was finally brought to an end in Denmark with the election of 1988.[131] In Sweden, the non-Socialist governments in power from 1976 to 1982 had neither the mandate nor, it seemed, the interest to alter the foreign policy course. Only the 1991 election of a non-Socialist coalition headed by the first Conservative Prime Minister since the 1930s signaled the beginning of three years of a new and expressly pro-American policy. But by then, the world was already a new, and unipolar, place.

---

130 Silva 1999, p. 50.
131 Fagerlund Knudsen 1990, pp. 114–115, Petersen 1991, pp. 90 ff

Part II.
The Nordic-Baltic Region in Unipolar Strategy

4. The Nordic-Baltic Region in Unipolar Strategy: Part I (1991–1996)

4.1 Subregions in the North

How was the Nordic region affected by unipolarity? How, and in what way, did developments in the international system influence the role of the Nordic region in US strategy? What strategic consequences did the new post-Cold War system, dominated by a single, or unipolar, power, have on Nordic security, on US policy toward the region, and on Baltic security as the region expanded eastward?[132]

As a consequence of the replacement of the bipolar Cold War with a system of unipolarity, the Nordic countries could no longer be considered, as they had been by some, as in a geopolitical location "between" the superpowers and the rival blocs. Neutral Sweden and Finland found themselves confronted with the logical question resulting from the survival of only one superpower: neutral between whom and regarding what? This geographic location "between" the superpowers had become of particular significance from the early 1980s on as the military perspective moved north, and the Kola Peninsula gained strategic prominence in Soviet planning (and subsequently, also in US strategy). As the Cold War ended, the "imbalance" of the security system in favor of the unipolar was reflected at the regional level, with a strong geopolitical as well as ideological move-

---

[132] This and the following chapters draw to a large extent on interviews conducted in Washington, DC, Stockholm, Copenhagen, Oslo, Helsinki, and Brussels.

ment in a transatlantic direction.[133] In addition, the regional area was reconstructed and extended, as it no longer made strategic sense to talk of Nordic security without also including the Baltic countries. A new entity, the Nordic-Baltic region, was created in Northern Europe as security concerns on both sides of the Baltic Sea merged.

The decline of the Soviet Union from its former superpower position to a reduced regional and great power role, led to major alterations in the geopolitical reality of Northern Europe. But developments on the eastern shore of the Baltic Sea continued to generate a considerable amount of concern for the Nordic countries in the unipolar world; initially, to an even greater extent than had been the case in previous decades, despite the positive political changes that Europe was experiencing. With the dramatic breakup of the Soviet empire and the sudden disappearance of the Warsaw Pact, the Baltic coastline, which had previously formed one massive and intransigent border between East and West, was rearranged, with a number of newly independent, small, and vulnerable states eager to find a place in the emerging security structure. In the southern part of the Baltic Sea, two giant European states returned to the Western community after years in the bipolar shadow: recently united Germany and Poland, liberated after decades under Soviet occupation and control. From a security perspective, it was soon evident that a whole new reality had descended upon the Nordic region and its subregions.

The way security in the Nordic region was now viewed by the US and NATO respectively, also underwent a drastic change. The region had always been located on the edge of the map as drawn by NATO, which focused mainly on the Central Front during close to five decades of bipolarity. With unipolarity, the Nordic region became relegated to an even more peripheral position as NATO no longer saw the main military challenge as emanating from the East. Thus, the Nordic region was seen in Brussels and Mons as ever more distant and peripheral with the removal of the Front, and a similar view emerged from Washington, where the superpower perspective had previously granted the region a much greater strategic significance than was usually the case in Alliance analysis. This was particularly true in times of tight bipolar tension, such as in the 1980s when the High North occupied a key position in US strategy.

With the advent of unipolarity, the region also experienced a substantial change in the numbers and location of its subregions. The hitherto dominant Northern Flank – or Front – saw a sharp decline in interest

---

133   See chapter 6 for a discussion on the political consequences of unipolarity on Nordic-Baltic security.

(though less so in actual strategic significance) from the outside world, when it no longer enjoyed the geopolitical vantage point (relatively speaking) next door to the American rival. At the same time, a new area rapidly surfaced, extending the region in an eastward direction and demanding the full attention of its Nordic neighbors. Shortly after the collapse of the bipolar system, the strategic center had effectively been transferred from the Northern Flank to the Baltic Sea area, where developments in the three newly liberated Baltic countries presented not only a new set of strategic problems, but also gave the region an additional subregion. From now on, the three Baltic countries would form an integral part of the region and place a whole new set of demands on security. The Baltic Sea region had now become "a single theatre of operation."[134]

In turn, other subregions experienced a strategic downgrading as a result of developments. The subregion previously centered on the Baltic Exits was basically removed from the strategic map with the disappearance of the Central Front to which it had been intimately connected. Instead, this area now constituted the western (primarily Danish-controlled) part of the new Baltic Sea region. A similar fate befell the Swedish–Finnish subregion, parts of which were absorbed by the new subregion in the Baltic. For nonaligned Sweden, which saw new political opportunities for itself in the Baltic Sea with the end of bipolarity, the remodeling of the map initiated vague though unrealistic dreams of a return of the historic – this time peaceful – Swedish role in the subregion. For equally nonaligned Finland, the Baltic area was next door and developments in the three countries, Estonia in particular, were of great strategic interest as Finland energetically sought to take advantage of the historic "window of opportunity" opened by unipolarity.

As a result, the five subregions existing in the Nordic region in the bipolar era were reduced to basically three in the unipolar system. One was the Northern Flank, with the Barents region as its central part, weakened because of diminished international (including American) interest, although hardly in terms of actual strategic relevance. During the first years of the unipolar system, many in Norway feared a return of this subregion to its earlier status as "the Forgotten Flank."[135] While the Kola Peninsula maintained the crucial position in military planning that it had enjoyed in Soviet times, the decrepit state of the military equipment stationed there (some of it relocated from the Central Front to Kola and Kaliningrad, an area of renewed military concern) gave a whole new meaning to the

---

134 Dörfer 1997, p. 92.
135 Tamnes 1997, pp. 7 ff.

concept of regional instability. The submarine accident off the Peninsula in the fall of 2000, when a Russian submarine, the *Kursk*, went under and its entire crew was abandoned to a brutal fate as a result of inaction in Moscow, was a terrifying reminder of the state of the military on the east side of the High North. NATO assistance in the rescue operation was first rejected, but in the end reluctantly accepted, with Norwegian and British experts assisting in bringing up the submarine.

Another subregion to survive the end of the Cold War was the one centered on the Atlantic Islands, which still provided a strategic bridge between the two continents. As Olafur Stephensen has argued from his national perspective, Iceland *is* and remains the transatlantic link due to its strategic location in the middle of the Atlantic Ocean, a location that makes the country "indispensable to an Atlantic Alliance in a time of crisis."[136] Nevertheless, this subregion too felt the consequences of the new times, with a reduced American presence on the Keflavik base (from which the US finally withdrew in 2006). After decades of opposing the American presence on the island, with imposed reductions in the number of US troops admitted and sharp limitations on American interaction with the locals, Iceland was of a different mind in the post-Cold War period and only reluctantly accepted the news from Washington.[137] The American base in Thule, Greenland, assumed a new assignment as early-warning was replaced by civil-military surveillance of space.

The final post-Cold War subregion, and the new addition to the group was thus the Baltic Sea subregion that occupied the strategic center of the region from the early 1990s on. This development was an obvious and immediate result of the unipolar system. But only when the US started to pay serious attention to what threatened to develop into a "gray zone" of regional instability and burdened with a highly uncertain security commitment from the West, did the Baltic Sea area emerge as an internationally recognized (sub)region in its own right. At that point, the strategic significance of the area had already been argued by local and other expertise for years. This delayed reaction demonstrates the unipolar system's monopoly in creating and defining regions and subregions (just as the bipolar rivalry defined the Nordic and other regions and subregions in the Cold War era).

---

136 Stephensen 1996, p. 1.
137 Zakheim 1998, p. 120.

4.2 The first phase: benevolent lack of interest (1991–1993)

4.2.1 Regional instability

The involuntary withdrawal of the Soviet Union from the bipolar rivalry also had obvious implications on the northern part of the European continent. The main strategic *raison d'etre* for the region, and in particular for the High North, had been its location immediately next door to the principal antagonist of the United States. While the dismantling of that threat alongside the entire Soviet Communist Empire removed the exceptional and often urgent state of tension from the region, in a paradoxical way it also created an increased perception of vulnerability among its actors, as a system of stable deterrence was replaced by a high degree of military instability and political uncertainty. This was most deeply felt in the case of Norway, still only a few miles from one of the world's largest collections of military equipment, although an increasingly rusty one, on the Kola Peninsula. Norway's feeling of marginalization was further strengthened as a result of the reorganization of NATO's command structure following the end of the Cold War, when Norway became militarily detached from the Continent.[138] The Scandinavian NATO allies were regrouped in separate commands: for Norway, the CINCNORTH command outside Oslo was replaced by the new AFNORTHWEST located in High Wycombe outside London, while Denmark came under the Central European Command (AFCENT) in Brunsum in the Netherlands.[139] As Norway witnessed these changes and the reduction of the US military presence in Europe, it turned to the intensified process of integration on the Continent in an effort to compensate for the loss of protection. This political choice was however rejected by the Norwegian electorate when it voted against a second proposal to join the European Community in 1994.

Before the international community had fully come to understand the dimension of the emerging disasters in former Yugoslavia, post-Cold War Europe was often described as being in a unique historic state of stability after a half-century of intense bipolar conflict. That was indeed a correct description of the area surrounding the highly militarized Central Front, where all signs of conflict had vanished seemingly overnight with the dis-

---

138 Tamnes gives a detailed account of the reorganizations of the command structures from a Norwegian perspective in 1997, pp. 9 f and 2004, pp. 37 ff.

139 Actually, the structure went through several changes, as CINCNORTH became CINCNORTHWEST/AFNORTH, which then became AFNORTHWEST. My thanks to Kjeld Hillingsø for this remark.

mantled rival armies. But in the northern part of the Continent, celebrations were mixed with a certain nostalgia for the military stability which had characterized the bipolar years – horrific as they were in other respects – but was now nowhere in sight.[140]

Compared to the situation on the Central Front, the Cold War had produced a relatively low level of military tension in Northern Europe for long periods of time. Although both the perceived and actual tension was considerable, especially in the High North, there had also been a general feeling of benign remoteness in relation to the rest of the world (especially in neutralist Sweden; much less so, for obvious reasons, in neighboring Finland). The movement of heavy Soviet and Warsaw Pact arms and military equipment from the Central Front to new locations on Kola and in Kaliningrad – a consequence of the weak protection of the flanks in the CFE Treaty – did not ease the strategic concerns taking hold in the Nordic region as the unipolar system was unfolding.[141] Moreover, while Russian troops pulled out of the Baltic region (maintaining a military presence in Latvia at the Skrunda radar site), naval units were transferred to already crowded Kaliningrad.[142] Apart from the emergence of new actors both in the east and south in the Baltic Sea, the new international system was characterized in the north by an increased sense of *uncertainty*, and, contrary to the feelings in Central Europe, with political and military *instability* dominating the neighborhood.

Much of this initial concern was caused by the uncertainty surrounding the ultimate fate of the crumbling Soviet neighbor. The collapse of the Soviet empire at the end of 1991 marked the conclusion of a dramatic development, which had begun in the Baltic Sea region as the three Baltic republics reclaimed their national independence. This historic development would have a major impact on Nordic stability and society. Conflict in some of the breakaway Soviet republics and between different nationalities; uncertainty as to the democratic foundation of the new Russia and severe economic troubles; fears of massive flows of illegal immigrants crossing the Baltic Sea; nuclear and military disarray; and international crime – all this and more created a situation of potential instability in the immediate Nordic neighborhood.

The destiny of the three small, vulnerable, and newly independent Baltic countries was of paramount interest and concern to the Nordic countries,

---

140 Waever (1992) analyzes "the Nordic nostalgia" which ensued in different parts of society upon the end of the Cold War.
141 See Tamnes 1997, pp. 3 ff. on the complexity of the CFE Treaty for the Northern flank.
142 Bildt 1994, pp. 76–77, Smith 2002, p. 14, Dörfer 1997, p. 6 f.

which had themselves enjoyed decades of political stability and success. But while developments in the Baltic region were early on seen by local actors as a critical litmus test of the evolving security structures, it took longer for the significance of Baltic security on the international system to be fully appreciated in the US.[143] The academic world saw a gradual increase in interest for the regional situation and the wider implications of this, with a growing number of publications and conferences on the subject from the early 1990s on.[144]

The US under the Bush I Administration was the 34th country to grant the Baltic States diplomatic recognition in 1991, beaten by Iceland as the first, with Denmark (which had however never diplomatically recognized the Soviet occupation of the Baltic countries) not far behind. This relative reluctance on the American part had disappointed the Baltic countries and added to the sense of mistrust in the political reliability of the United States.[145] In a similar fashion, for years after the end of the Cold War, visitors to the State Department and the Pentagon encountered a benevolent lack of interest for regional security when requesting a US analysis of the situation in the northern part of Europe. The prevailing, though friendly, response was that as a region of peaceful and stable democracies with little cause for concern for their security – an analysis which was indeed true for the Nordic but definitely not for the Baltic countries – this could hardly be seen as neither an academic nor political priority when more urgent problems were erupting in the southeastern corner of Europe. Only a small number of individuals in the Administration took a personal interest in this issue; one desk officer at the State Department resigned as a result of the delayed diplomatic recognition of the newly independent Baltic States.[146]

Foreign policy was a low-level priority for the Clinton Administration, which took office in January 1993, with the new president focusing on economic issues and taking a full year before he embarked on his first presidential trip overseas. In the first half of the 1990s, political and diplomatic circles in the US were absorbed by two separate issues: one, how (or rather, how not) to respond to the exceptionally nasty Balkan crisis which was rapidly escalating to full-scale war; and two, how to deal with

---

143 Bildt 1994, p. 72 ff.
144 Early studies were published by Brundtland and Snider 1993, Cambone 1993.
145 Swedish diplomat Lars Peter Fredén provides a detailed insider's perspective on this period, and describes the Americans as often "naïve" with regards to Baltic-Russian relations (and with regards to Russia generally), and with a lacking understanding of the Baltic countries. See for example 2006, pp. 240, 252.
146 According to a person who worked closely with this office at the time.

the intense knocking on NATO's door by former Warsaw Pact members, without exhausting and overextending the American security commitment. The situation in the Baltic Sea region appeared at best to be at the very end of the list of priorities.

In this early phase of US policy, Nordic security was still seen as separate from the situation on the eastern shore of the Baltic Sea. The subregion covering the entire Baltic area would emerge only at a later stage as Washington identified a gray zone dilemma threatening regional – and international – security (see *Second Phase*, below). Although an extensive program of US assistance was presented to the Baltic countries, the bulk of American involvement at this stage was performed by the use of Nordic proxy. The successful personal involvement by Swedish Prime Minister Carl Bildt, resulting in the military pullout by Russia from the Baltic countries, is a prominent example of Nordic–American cooperation for the Baltic cause at this time.

The new government headed by Conservative Prime Minister Carl Bildt came to power determined to turn the focus of Swedish foreign and security policy around to Europe and the Nordic-Baltic neighborhood, after decades when the Third World was the number one priority in Stockholm.[147] According to Swedish sources, the Prime Minister was asked by the American president to "please take care of things" in the (sub)region on American behalf, and to pursue issues which the US itself could, or would not, get involved with for a variety of reasons. As Dörfer explains, the Bildt government had made "its special task the improvement of the security situation of the Baltic and thereby of Sweden, as well." US–Swedish cooperation continued as a new president arrived in the White House: "The Clinton Administration coming into power in January 1993 encouraged the Swedish quiet diplomacy and laid the groundwork with Moscow while the three Baltic States themselves worked out the details."[148]

But Sweden was not the only country engaged in the diplomatic undertakings leading up to the withdrawal of Russian troops: Finland, enjoying special ties with Estonia, and Denmark were both involved in this process. Also, this and similar arrangements did not preclude direct American involvement, such as when President Clinton put American pressure on President Yeltsin by co-authoring "stiff notes" with German Prime Minister Herman Kohl to remind the Russian leader of his promise to withdraw Russian troops from Baltic territory (which eventually happened in

---

147 See Dahl (Nilsson) 1991a.
148 Dörfer 1997, p. 78.

1994).[149] The polite reserve and a more disengaged attitude toward Nordic-Baltic issues were however more characteristic of the US approach to the region in the early 1990s. As Fredén notes, the superpower had a lot of other things on its mind – in particular relations with Russia, the number one priority.[150]

4.3   The second phase: a Baltic dilemma (1994–1997)

4.3.1   A gray zone

The Brussels Summit in January 1994 launched the NATO Partnership for Peace program aimed at pacifying the impatient group of former Warsaw Pact countries keen on joining NATO. The PfP had originally consisted of just a basic idea, with actual content gradually added on. The Danish government, passing on some of its early experience of working in the Baltic region to the new NATO program, provided some of the content.[151] While one or two Americans may have envisioned Baltic membership in NATO as the ultimate goal at this stage, the general idea of the PfP was to delay membership for the European candidates in general (and the Balts in particular), not as a waiting room for NATO. Similarly, while it was explicitly stated in the PfP program that partnership could indeed eventually lead to formal membership, including Article Five protection once the requirements for democratic and civil–military changes were met, it was evident in the case of the three vulnerable Baltic States that the US and NATO were neither "ready nor willing" (to use NATO vocabulary) to admit them as formal members for quite some time.[152]

The Brussels Summit revealed a slightly more engaged American attitude toward involvement in European security than in the previous years, including a gradual US acknowledgment of the troublesome situation in northern Europe. But the American perspective on Nordic-Baltic security was still primarily characterized by a reluctance to confront the problems head on. The Baltic regions firmly remained in the "too hard to handle" category in US foreign policy.[153]

---

149 Smith 2002, p. 32.
150 Fredén 2006, pp. 252 ff. This view is confirmed in Bildt 1994.
151 According to Ambassador Per Carlsen, who worked closely with Foreign Minister Hans Haekkerup at the time.
152 Zakheim 1997, p. 8.
153 Asmus 1997b, p. 42.

This American reluctance prevailed in spite of the fact – or precisely because of it – that the Baltic countries found themselves in an environment undoubtedly much more hostile than the small group of Central European countries quickly singled out as the leading membership candidates. Thinly veiled threats of Russian armed intervention had been made as late as 1994, after an incident close to the Latvian capital, Riga – one of two places where Soviet-led massacres had taken place only three years earlier (the other place was Vilnius, Lithuania). The possessive Russian attitude to the countries and people of the areas referred to by Moscow as its "near abroad" was the source of major preoccupation for the democracies in the Nordic region that shared a border with Russia. Only after the completion of the drawn-out Russian military withdrawal from the three sovereign Baltic republics in August, 1994 were the Nordic countries allowed to relax some, although a number of problems relating to the military installations and Russian minorities remained on the agenda.

Looking back on that period, Ron Asmus, then analyst at RAND and later appointed Deputy Assistant Secretary of State, recalls that:

> ... in 1993, 1994, 1995, there was a real concern that the NATO enlargement debate was solely or primarily focused on East-Central Europe. And there was a fear that this region was being neglected, forgotten, or was somehow a lesser priority either to the United States or to the Alliance as a whole. The fear was, somehow, that the Baltic States or this region would be left out of the new security structure we were trying to build – would be left behind in some kind of gray zone.[154]

The hesitant attitude toward the Baltic region was a result of American fear of violent Russian reaction to the idea of enlargement in the former Soviet territory. The Nordic countries shared this concern, although most of them did not share the conclusions drawn in Washington. Russia finally joined the former neutrals and the Baltic countries in signing up as a partner in the PfP program after a lengthy period of obstruction, but an endless stream of contradictory – mostly negative – statements kept emanating out of Moscow on the subject of NATO enlargement. Notwithstanding the difficulties and the threats formulated by Russian extremists, who only served to strengthen the Baltic determination, the three small states relentlessly continued to push for membership in the Alliance. But while NATO remained the only organization with military credibility, as viewed by the Baltic countries also seeking membership in the EU, the Alliance was far from ready to include the former Soviet republics in the group of official candidates. American and NATO reluctance to attend to the problems in

---

154 Asmus in Kruzick and Kornfehl 1998, p. 27.

the region left the Baltic countries in an uncomfortable and vulnerable situation, with only the vague and inadequate security arrangements of the PfP to lean on, corresponding only to the consultation mechanisms of Article 4 of the Washington Treaty.

The emergence of a potential *gray zone* with unclear security commitments and an uncertain division of responsibility on the eastern shore of the Baltic Sea after a first round of enlargement had included the three Visegrad countries as new NATO members, was a scenario dreaded in Northern Europe. To some – in particular in Washington – such an outcome was seen as almost unavoidable.

At the Pentagon and the NATO HQ in Mons, military experts brutally dismissed the small and vulnerable Baltic countries on former Soviet territory as simply *indefensible*, a prediction that, critics argued, ran the obvious risk of becoming a self-fulfilling prophecy. In 1994, maps could still be found in the Pentagon so out of date that a visitor had to fill out the contours of the independent Baltic States' borders with Russia.[155] This may indeed have contributed to the pessimistic predictions from these quarters. Nevertheless, a small number of individuals at the State and Defense Departments and the White House took a personal interest in Baltic security, and established close and cherished contacts with their Nordic and Baltic counterparts in the process. In addition, a new office opened at the State Department in 1994, as the Nordic desk absorbed the three Baltic countries.[156] Nordic-Baltic issues also gradually merged as the two regions were included in the same diplomatic training program at the State Department's Foreign Service Institute (the very first Baltic Area Studies course had started already in 1992 with only a handful of "students").

A certain discrepancy existed between official rhetoric and informal American analysis. In spite of the gloomy analysis of the situation in the region presented in many offices in Washington, President Clinton promised at a historic visit to Riga in July, 1994 that the US would "stand with you, we will help you, we will be partners so that your nation can be forever free."[157] The president's wording, describing the relationship in terms of a "partnership", was no doubt a deliberate effort to avoid the delicate issue of NATO membership. From an American perspective, Alliance membership remained an unrealistic policy for the three Baltic States, however sensitive their security situation (or rather, precisely because of this vulnerability and the geopolitical realities of the Baltic countries).

155 According to Peeter Luksep, former member of Parliament of both Sweden and Estonia.
156 Tamnes 1997, p. 13.
157 Bildt 1994, p. 83.

The visit by the American president was intended only as a general show of support for the Baltic struggle, not as a prelude to formal commitments by the Americans beyond the inadequate Article 4.

4.3.2 Regionalization of security

From 1995, a number of proposals started to surface from various parts of the academic and political worlds that, from widely differing perspectives, had started to take an interest in the security issues of the Baltic Sea region. All suggested ways to exit the paralyzing gray zone mentality that dominated analysis, and the view, firmly held by the US and NATO, of the Baltic region as being an insolvable security dilemma. Most proposals pointed in the direction of some form of *regionalization* of security as a solution to the problem, with the Nordic countries assuming special responsibilities for their small neighbors to the east. In response, regional actors warned against a diluted role for NATO or the US, or of any plan that would establish a separate area outside the mainstream of transatlantic security.[158]

The theme of these proposals coincided with the general trend toward political regionalization at the time. It was obvious that the security of a rapidly expanding "Europe" could no longer be dealt with through a single, coherent set of instruments, as had been the case during the Cold War, even though Europe had been split in two parts at that time. Instead, under US guidance, NATO had started to apply a new approach to security, dividing the Continent and its increasingly diverse problems regionally. The strategically most demanding regions by far at this time were the Balkans and the Mediterranean region, with the Baltic region much lower on the list of priorities. With this conceptual compartmentalization of security the unipolar power was hoping to avoid overextension in an international system that was constantly calling for its attention.

In many instances, however, the various ideas for a regionalization of security, presented in a multitude of shapes and fashions, seemed to suggest a reduced involvement on the part of the one remaining superpower. That made the whole concept much less attractive from a European, and especially Northern European, perspective. It often remained unclear whether a regional division of labor should be seen as a means to enable the US to slowly withdraw its engagement and presence, or simply as a scheme for making the provision of security more effective. Contrary to

---

158 Asmus 1997b, p. 44. Also see Dörfer 1997, 81 ff. for a discussion of the various proposals for regionalization at this time.

the initial fears surrounding the discussion, it soon became evident that regionalization in the Baltic Sea area would actually result in an increase, rather than a reduction, of US involvement. The study that would pave the way for this new American approach to regional security in the Baltic Sea was the result of a concerted effort by a small number of US analysts entertaining a particular interest in the region.

Proposals on the subject emerged both from within the Nordic-Baltic region itself and from the outside. Two prominent Nordic political and diplomatic personalities each presented their solution to the problems surrounding regional security. Finnish ambassador and security expert Max Jakobson's proposal that the Nordic countries extend a similar kind of security umbrella over the Baltic States that nonaligned Sweden and Finland themselves had enjoyed throughout the Cold War (a suggestion which required that the two Nordic countries join NATO) stirred up debate quite a bit, as had presumably been Jakobson's intention and hope.[159]

In 1996, the former Prime Minister of Sweden, Carl Bildt, then high representative of the EU in Bosnia and well acquainted with the practical aspects of peacekeeping, suggested a regional subdivision of the Partnership for Peace program. Such a *Northern PfP* would, as Bildt envisioned it, serve as a structure for cooperation among the Baltic and Nordic countries, with special responsibilities for regional security within the already established PfP frame. Cooperation would extend to the military level through the organization of joint Nordic-Baltic forces for deployment in international operations and peacekeeping task, such as the one that was carried out in Bosnia. This model did not require a change of doctrine for the nonaligned Nordic states, at least not in the short-term, but was seen by the author himself (although is not known as a great advocate of Swedish NATO membership) as a practical and pragmatic way to deal with the rapidly approaching *fait accompli* of the three Baltic States being excluded from the first round of NATO membership; "a good alternative to an enlarged NATO in our part of the world," in the former Prime Minister's words.[160] In many ways, the idea resembled the extensive net of practical cooperation that would soon emerge across the Baltic Sea.

From outside the region itself, former British Foreign Minister Douglas Hurd addressed the general security problems confronting the Alliance, Baltic stability included, at a talk at the *International Institute for Strategic*

---

[159] See Jakobson 1998, especially pp. 140–146, and interview in *Dagens Nyheter*, July 5, 1997.

[160] Bildt, 1996, p. 18 ff. Carl Bildt has argued in favor of Swedish membership in NATO only once, in an op-ed co-authored with former Danish Foreign Minister Uffe Ellemann-Jensen, (*Dagens Nyheter*, February 3, 2003).

Studies in London in late March 1996.¹⁶¹ Contrary to Jakobson and others who saw Finland and Sweden as future members of NATO, but not unlike the Bildt proposal, Hurd suggested a nonaligned pact in the Baltic Sea region. Though critical of Nordic neutrality, Hurd nevertheless proposed a scheme through which the two Nordic nonaligned countries would be able to return the favors rendered them by NATO throughout the Cold War, by providing the three Baltic countries with an enhanced level of regional security. By doing that, Hurd was hoping to avoid extending guarantees to the Baltic States through NATO or even the EU. At a conference on the Swedish island of Visby in the summer of 1995, German Defense Minister Volker Ruhe had made a similar case, arguing for close security links with the Nordic countries as a substitute for Baltic membership in NATO.¹⁶²

Although arriving at such diverse conclusions and coming from widely differing sets of assumptions, all proposals presented in the mid-1990s were searching for a solution to the anticipated dilemma in the Baltic Sea: how to provide the three Baltic States with an acceptable level of security without provoking Russia to overreact and thereby spoil the entire project of regional stability in the process. Most notably, all proposals (including the one by RAND Corporation to which we turn below) tied Baltic security closely to Nordic security, and provided the Nordic states with special responsibilities – directly or indirectly on behalf of American interests – toward what was now clearly in practical terms (if not yet in official policies) becoming a new subregion in the north.

However, the proposal that provoked the greatest amount of attention and which would also enjoy a considerable impact on US policy, was the one presented by a group of analysts at RAND Corporation. Having previously been concerned with more general questions of NATO enlargement, the group turned in the mid-1990s to the dilemma about to surface in the Baltic region after a first round of new members had been accepted into the Alliance. The RAND proposal outlined a multifaceted strategy that involved the US and NATO (but not, critics argued, to a sufficient degree), while also taking into account the many complexities surrounding the regional situation and Russian sensitivities.

The main components of the study were: a) emphasis on the need to encourage political and economic reform in the Baltic countries, as well as policies of cooperation in defense and security policy-related issues among themselves (aiming at the establishment of national subscription armies

---

161 Hurd, 1996.
162 *Frankfurte Allgemeine Zeitung*, June 20, 1995.

modeled on the Finnish army); b) rapid EU membership for the Baltic States, ideally in concert with Baltic accession to NATO; c) increased Nordic-Baltic cooperation as "a complementary pillar and not as a substitute" to US involvement; and finally, d) a credible "open door" Alliance strategy on membership. In addition, the report recommended that NATO embark on an intensified dialogue with Russia.[163] This strategy, described as an effort to overcome the factors that worked against Baltic membership in the Alliance, was presented as having multiple advantages:[164]

> This policy buys time for the Baltic countries to try to build political support for their own objectives, for the West to develop a new political and strategic situation in Europe. At the same time, this strategy candidly acknowledges the real obstacles to eventual Baltic membership in the Alliance and tries to develop strategies to alleviate them.[165]

As this second phase of US policy drew to a close, the political impact that the RAND study (a draft of which had been circulated in Washington and the Nordic capitals for quite some time prior to publication) had on the American approach to the gray zone dilemma would become quite substantial. The impact was clear with the appointment in 1997 of its main author, Ronald Asmus, to the position of Deputy Assistant Secretary of State at the US State Department. In the Nordic and Baltic capitals, the appointment of Asmus was interpreted as a positive signal, and a definite indication that the strategic significance of the region in the new and unipolar world was finally acknowledged in Washington. To Finland and Sweden, the RAND proposal served to calm their previous concerns that the burden of Baltic security be placed on their militarily and politically inadequate shoulders (as everyone, NATO and Washington included, realized all too well, and as Baltic officials were inclined to point out). To Denmark, it was a confirmation of the value and significance of the intense contacts that Asmus and his colleagues had had with the Danish Defense Ministry when drafting the proposed policy, and of the role the Danish government had designed for itself as special protector of Baltic issues within NATO.

---

163 Asmus and Nurrick, 1996, pp. 129–139, Asmus 1997a, p. 12.
164 Asmus 1997a, pp. 12, 15.
165 Asmus and Nurrick 1996, p. 139.

4.3.3 Intra-Nordic rivalries

Under the firm guidance of Defense Minister Hækkerup, Denmark had assumed a de facto leading role within NATO in the Baltic Sea region, while also becoming the prime, and in the early stages the only, advocate within NATO of "second round" Baltic membership in the Alliance.[166] When first officially unveiled in the Copenhagen Declaration in the spring of 1997, Danish policy, strongly in favor of NATO enlargement to the three Baltic States, was reported to have caused quite some irritation in Washington.[167] But it was later generally acknowledged that it was mainly due to the persistent efforts by Denmark that the Baltic countries were specifically mentioned in the final document from the Madrid summit in 1997 as potential candidates for membership in the next round of enlargement (see below for the next phase).[168] As Danish Foreign Minister Niels Helveg-Petersen recalls, Denmark and the US were the only two member countries supporting the idea of Baltic membership in NATO up until 2000, only two years before invitations were issued to the Baltic countries to start negotiations on membership in the Alliance.[169] After that, the idea grew gradually more popular within the Alliance.[170]

The practical advantages enjoyed by Denmark as the sole country in the region to combine NATO- and EU-membership were crucial for the implementation of the ambitious Danish program. As a result of Danish determination to come to the aid of the Baltic countries, an effort in which the American Ambassador to Copenhagen, Edward Elson, enthusiastically assisted, a number of activities were embarked upon under Danish guidance. Denmark quickly positioned itself as the leading force in training the Baltic military, slowly attracting the support of the other Nordic countries as well as that of Germany, France, the Netherlands, and the US. Numerous military cooperation schemes and agreements were produced between the Nordic countries and the Baltic States, some of it under Danish auspices. Danish activism in the Baltic Sea included the creation and training of the Baltic peacekeeping battalion, the BALTBAT, training and integrating Baltic platoons into the Danish battalion in former Yugoslavia, and as initiator of the BALTSEA donor coordination group.[171]

---

166 Asmus 1997a, p. 11.

167 Zakheim 1997, p. 18, Dörfer 1997, p. 78.

168 See the document from the Madrid Summit (1997).

169 According to a statement by the former Estonian Foreign Minister, Trivimi Velliste, in Copenhagen in May 2002.

170 See Asmus 2002, pp. 228 ff. for a description of the "Baltic challenge" to US policy and NATO.

171 Zakheim 1997, p. 14. Also *Lessons learned from the BALTBAT project* (2001).

As Zakheim, however, noted "Washington [did] not ... view Denmark as having a monopoly in supporting the interests of the Baltic States, nor [did] it assign Denmark any particular leadership role above those of its other Nordic neighbors."[172] As a matter of fact, the US went to considerable lengths to balance the praise it distributed among the various Nordic countries for their efforts in the region. According to some sources, there were times when Danish policy in the region was actually seen as a bit too determined for the American taste. At one point it was described as an example of "excessive enthusiasm."[173]

After an initial period when Denmark seemed to have enjoyed more or less sole control, Sweden entered the scene with regional ambitions of its own, reactivating in the process old historic rivalries (this time friendly) between the two countries. Both countries felt they had been specifically encouraged by the US to play prominent roles, and to exploit their respective backgrounds and positions. Although they were pursuing different agendas due to the discrepancies in security doctrines, both were actively seeking recognition from Washington for their work, as well as acknowledgement as the prime actor in the region. This situation required extensive diplomatic skills on the American side. It was pointed out from Washington that:

> [t]he United States does not want to alienate either Copenhagen or Stockholm. Nor does it wish, in any way, to lessen the enthusiasm of either. It has therefore gone to considerable lengths not only to praise both, but also ... to stress the importance of all Nordic efforts to strengthen Baltic sovereignty and generate regional cooperation.[174]

While Denmark acted from the vantage point enjoyed by a card-holding member of NATO and the EU (but not the WEU), nonaligned Sweden aspired to attain a level of political importance that would match its geographical size and what was seen as the country's general significance in the region. The historic role as a regional superpower served as obvious inspiration for Swedish policy in the Baltic Sea. But even though Stockholm emphasized the special and unique role in international affairs that, according to the Social Democratic government back in power in late 1994, only a nonaligned country could perform, there were limits to what

---

172 Zakheim 1997, 15–16.
173 Ibid, 1997, p. 18.
174 Ibid, 1997, p. 16.

even an ambitious but still nonaligned Sweden could and would do.[175]

The impromptu proclamation in early 1996 by Prime Minister Göran Persson that "the cause of the Baltic States is our cause" had immediately raised expectations and interest in Washington and elsewhere for a substantial Swedish contribution to problem-solving in the region. But any kind of military support other than within the framework of the PfP had been out of reach at the time; even an artillery gun used to salute the Swedish King on an official visit to Latvia had to be immediately returned to Sweden in order not to be interpreted as Swedish arms support across the Baltic Sea.[176] Initially, nonaligned Sweden chose to rely on the option offered by the increasingly fashionable concept of "soft security." Eventually, though, Sweden would emerge as the number one provider in Europe of financial and military assistance to the three Baltic States.[177] When the American "super diplomat" Richard Holbrooke (who had expressed considerable skepticism at the idea of Baltic membership in NATO) accepted a Swedish invitation to become a board member of the Baltic Sea Council, set up by the regional governments after a Danish–German initiative in an effort to attract foreign investment and environmental and other assistance to the Baltic States, it was seen as a great success for nonaligned diplomacy and an indication of the country's steadily improving relations with the US. From an American perspective, the extensive diplomatic and economic program to stabilize the Baltic region also presented Sweden with a channel to return some of the favors granted to the country during the Cold War, when covert agreements for assistance were arranged between nonaligned Sweden and a number of NATO allies, chief among them the US.[178]

The visit by the Swedish Premier to the White House in August, 1996 was described by national media as a great success for Göran Persson personally as well as for his country.[179] The trip generated high hopes for a return visit to Stockholm by President Clinton in connection with the Madrid summit in the summer of 1997, which in turn would have been

---

175 See Dahl and Hillmer 2002a for a study of the active foreign policies of NATO and nonaligned countries.

176 According to a person present at the ceremony.

177 Smith 2002, p. 39–40, also Dörfer 1997, p. 89 (fn 40).

178 *Svenska Dagbladet*, August 28, 1996. For information on the secret agreements with NATO, see SOU 1994:11.

179 For example in *Svenska Dagbladet*, August 24, 1996.

a first by an American president in power. The great expectations for a visit at this specific time originated in part from the personal friendship between the American ambassador to Stockholm, Thomas Siebert, and the president, dating back to the time when they were both students at Georgetown University.

In the end the president traveled, however, not to Stockholm but to Copenhagen following the Madrid Summit. While the president's travel plans resulted in poorly veiled disappointment in the Swedish capital (and very limited Swedish media coverage of Bill Clinton's program in the neighboring country), reactions were all the more jubilant in Copenhagen, where US Ambassador Edward Elson (himself of Lithuanian background) had been actively campaigning for a presidential visit. There, the visit was seen as final proof that Danish efforts to promote Baltic security had been a great success and appreciated by the Americans.[180] But sources at the State Department recommended Sweden not to interpret the selection of capitals as offensive. Instead, it was presented as basically a matter of political logistics. It would, State Department officials politely emphasized, have been quite difficult for the President to visit yet another neutral capital after the Helsinki Summit with President Yeltsin earlier the same year, an event which had helped to ease some of the tensions surrounding the first round of NATO enlargement. Also, it was said to make sense for the president to travel from the summit meeting in Madrid to a NATO ally, rather than to a country that, however enthusiastic a PfP participant, did not belong among the then 16 NATO members.

Finland was less visible in this process than regional activists Denmark and Sweden, but the Finnish government too received ample praise from State Department officials for its constructive approach to problem-solving in the region. All three Baltic countries were recipients of Finnish assistance, but the bulk of it was provided to Estonia, with special emphasis on its efforts to construct a credible military force.[181] Each Baltic country was "adopted" by a Nordic country, with Finland focusing on Estonia, Sweden on Latvia, and Denmark on Lithuania, with positive trade relations developing in the process. Unlike equally nonaligned Sweden, often described as suffering from a heavy dose of nostalgia for its neutral past, and whose

---

180 Danish TV for example dedicated the whole day to the President's visit, airing the speech in its entirety. Clinton was enthusiastically greeted also during his first of many return visits to Copenhagen as ex-president in the spring of 2001 (while a last minute change of meeting facility had to be arranged in Stockholm a few weeks later, due to lack of public interest).
181 Smith 2002, pp. 40–41.

tendency for moralizing could still provoke deep feelings of resentment in Washington, the extraordinary efforts by Finland in the late 1990s to reach a workable solution to regional security were actually such that the country amounted to "a 17th member" of the Alliance in US eyes. That was a title often assigned to Sweden during the Cold War.

However, the election in March 2000 of Tarja Halonen as President of the Republic would (as would her re-election in 2006) put a temporary end to any plans or dreams entertained among the country's security elite for Finnish membership in NATO. Many expected an application to be filed for Finnish membership in the first enlargement round during the tenure of her predecessor, President Ahtisaari, but any such expectations had to be postponed, in part because of Finland's entry into the EU.[182] Instead, Finnish warnings in April 2000 and August 2001 against Baltic membership in NATO created the impression that Finland was the only Western country to share Moscow's opposition to NATO enlargement.[183] That impression was reversed after the September 2001 bilateral meeting between Presidents Halonen and Putin, when the Finnish President finally made clear that she saw Baltic membership in NATO as basically a matter of not "if" but "when".[184]

While Sweden, Denmark, and Finland were engaged in a neighborly competition for a prominent position and influence in the Baltic Sea region, Norway was conspicuously absent, focusing instead on maintaining a presence in the Balkans. The two Scandinavian NATO members applied opposing strategies after the end of the Cold War; Denmark, enjoying a vastly improved strategic situation in the unipolar world, used "the new NATO" to its advantage as the former footnote country turned activist in the Baltic Sea region, advocating Baltic membership in NATO from an early stage. Meanwhile, Norway clung to the old concept of collective defense, and only reluctantly approved the new 1991 Strategic Concept. From Oslo's perspective, NATO was seen primarily as an instrument for integrating Russia into Europe, with the need for dialogue with Moscow always at the top of the Norwegian NATO agenda. Norway came across as a traditionalist ally, which managed to muster only tepid support for the Baltic cause, or for NATO enlargement generally.[185]

The American ambition regarding the rivalry of the Nordic countries was evident in the 1996 *Baltic Action Plan*. The BAP was yet another

---

182 Ries 2002, p. 216 f.
183 Ries 2001, 215, 220.
184 Smith 2002, pp. 40–41; Ries 2002, pp. 215, 220.
185 Dörfer 1997, p. 36 ff., Smith 2002, pp. 42–42.

attempt (as was previously the PfP) to deal with the intensive knocking on NATO's door for which the Clinton Administration was far from ready, although fully aware of the need for a Baltic strategy and wanting in due course the full integration of the Baltic countries into the West. Unveiled shortly before the 1996 US presidential elections, it was quickly nicknamed the "Baltic Electoral Plan."[186]

The second phase of US–Nordic/Baltic relations was thus characterized by a growing awareness among actors, including those outside the Nordic region, of the risks inherent in the emergence of a gray zone in the Baltic Sea region. Although American policy was still primarily a matter of gradually strengthened rhetorical support for the Baltic cause, the region clearly benefited from the debate started in 1996 as a number of proposals were presented on how to solve the gray zone dilemma. As those proposals gained wider attention, it became increasingly obvious that the issue of stability and security in the region presented "... one of the most difficult and politically sensitive issues in the entire enlargement debate, and although these countries are small they have a disproportionate impact on Russian politics, on American politics and on relations between NATO and Russia."[187] The then-Swedish Ambassador in Washington was one of many to voice a suspicion that one reason for the enhanced US support for the Baltic cause was that Washington felt it had to do something to improve the situation in the region after having agreed to the CFE treaty in 1990 that dramatically reduced regional security by accepting massive transfers of Russian troops close to the Baltic borders.[188]

As the centrality of the Baltic subregion for the creation of a peaceful and cooperative "new world order," and for the enlargement of NATO, became a general concern at various think tanks and institutions during this period, the analysis presented by the RAND team was instrumental in bringing US policy forward in the region. But the message from the Pentagon – aware of the fact that two Nordic countries maintained a policy of nonalignment – was that "while we are happy with the efforts of our Nordic friends, we don't want the Baltic States to become a Nordic sub-region."[189] Indeed, to rely on Nordic leadership and expect the regional actors to assume the burden of responsibility for the security of

---

186 "Baltic Action Plan", published by the US Mission to NATO in February 1997; Asmus, 2002, pp. 228 ff., 301 f. Also Zakheim 1998, p. 115 f.
187 Asmus 1997a, p. 11.
188 Interview with former Swedish Ambassador to Washington, DC, Henrik Liljegren, *Svenska Dagbladet*, August 28, 1996. Also see his memoirs, Liljegren 2004.
189 Cited in Zakheim 1997, p. 19.

their Baltic neighbors, as most of the proposals had, was totally unrealistic. However, in the next and third phase of US–Nordic-Baltic relations it became clear that the three Baltic countries had become a fully integrated part of the Nordic region in terms of security; from now on, it would no longer be possible to separate the security of one part of the region from the others.

5. The Nordic-Baltic Region in Unipolar Strategy: Part II (1997–2007)

5.1 The third phase: unipolar determination (1997–1998)

5.1.1 The Nordic-Baltic region post-Madrid

During the third phase of unipolar policy it became clear that the United States had indeed come to fully realize the strategic significance of the Baltic Sea region, as well as the severe consequences, which a collapse of regional security could have on global affairs. After the previous period, when the gray zone dilemma had exercised an almost paralyzing effect in Washington, the third period, starting with the Madrid Summit in the summer of 1997, was characterized by an increasingly strong American determination to move policy in the region forward, in order to reach a durable solution to the security dilemma surrounding the Baltic Sea. The Clinton Administration, as it moved into its second term in office, showed signs of taking a greater interest in the world, after a first tenure controlled by domestic and economic issues. The situation in the Balkans had been forcefully – though reluctantly – dealt with and at least temporarily settled, although far from resolved as the Kosovo campaign would soon demonstrate. US policy had assumed a less introverted outlook.

The 1997 annual conference on Baltic security arranged by the American Embassy in Stockholm demonstrated the intellectual and political evolution that had taken place over a relatively short period of time. While the conference the year before had been dominated by sober warnings of emerging gray zones, the one in 1997 was conducted in a much more positive and constructive spirit.[190] During the third unipolar phase, a number of the academic and political ideas that had been introduced during the second phase were implemented in American policy, in some instances by the very same people who had originally formulated some of the ideas. A change in rhetoric to a less evasive and more assertive tone followed.

This period was also characterized by the abandonment of the overly cautious "Russia first" strategy, whose main proponent had been Strobe Talbott, in which the overwhelming concern for developments in Russia had relegated regional security to a secondary position. Although the objections still invariably raised by Russia were in no way ignored in Washington – proved by the signing of the NATO–Russian Founding Act preceding the Madrid Summit – the American ambition now was to have Russia "get bored with NATO and NATO enlargement," as formulated by then Secretary of State Madeleine Albright. Early in her tenure, Albright had traveled to Moscow and Vilnius on her journey to assure Moscow of the harmlessness of US and NATO policy.[191] Top officials at the State Department were now hoping that the idea of including a few additional states into NATO, following the entry of the three Visegrad countries in 1999, would gradually become less disturbing to Moscow.

NATO's Madrid Summit in the summer of 1997 thus marked the formal start of a new, more activist American policy in the region. That the three Baltic States were explicitly mentioned in the final document as possible candidate countries for a second round of enlargement caused joyous celebrations in the Nordic-Baltic region. The gradually enhanced US interest for the region during the second and third phases was at least in part a response to the explicit Nordic and Baltic requests for American assistance and support, drawing Washington into the process, and from the academic pursuit of the topic at various American think tanks. In the region itself, Denmark could – and happily did – take special credit for forcefully pursuing the issue of Baltic Sea security, placing a massive amount of pressure on their American – and European – colleagues in NATO, and constantly arguing the merits of Baltic inclusion in NATO.

5.1.2   Northern and Baltic initiatives

Following the successful conclusion of the 1997 Madrid Summit, the US State Department prepared a *Northern European Initiative,* which outlined a detailed strategy for the Nordic-Baltic region. The initiative departed

---

190 As noted by Asmus in his speech at the 1997 conference (Asmus 1997b, p. 42).
191 Cited in Asmus 1997b, p. 42.

from the points made in the *Survival* article penned a few years earlier by the RAND group.[192] Among them was Ron Asmus, whose move to the State Department reflected the general transition of the Nordic-Baltic issue from being an intellectual pursuit of a limited group of think tank enthusiasts to increasingly become a policy priority in Washington, DC. The basic idea behind the newly energized initiative was to create a positive and constructive policy for the region, rather than to focus solely on avoiding the emergence of a gray zone.[193] The Hanseatic League was often mentioned in this context, in spite of the many differences between Hanseatic times and the mid- to late 1990s. In the initiative, a reference was made to the importance of tradition: the policy, it said, "reflects a yearning or a desire to return to a greater sense of normality in the region after all these years of division."[194]

To that effect, a three-track strategy was presented in the policy paper first referred to as the *Northern European Initiative* and later renamed the *Northeast Europe Initiative* (NEI). The first part of this strategy emphasized the need for intensified US efforts to help the Baltic States help themselves become the strongest possible candidates for integration in Western structures, NATO included – in other words, more or less what the Nordic countries had been busy doing for the past few years. Second, a policy of support was outlined for cooperation between Northern Europe and Northern Russia, finding ways and means for joint regional projects while leaving Russian–American disagreement on NATO enlargement behind. And third, efforts were suggested to strengthen Nordic–US relations while also extending the link to a wider group of actors such as Poland, Germany, France, the UK, and the EU. The role of the US, as explained by Asmus, would be to function as a "value-added," and to step in where it could make a difference.[195]

This policy, it was stressed, should not be seen as a US policy of *regionalization* in the sense discussed previously, leaving the bulk of responsibility to regional actors while withdrawing to a more remote American position. Rather, the aim was now to jointly reach a state of normalization, to the point where the Baltic Sea region would be just another part of Europe.[196] Critics however argued that the whole concept would primarily be seen

192 Asmus, Kugler, and Larrabee 1993.
193 Asmus, 1997b p. 3. Cf. speech by Ambassador Lyndon L. Olson, Jr. at the conference organized by the Swedish Atlantic Council in February 26, 1998.
194 Speech by Ron Asmus in Helsinki 1997, published in *Baltic Sea Region Brief*, p. 26.
195 Asmus 1997b, p. 4.
196 Ibid.

as just a rather unrealistic act of US good will, which in addition suffered from a number of obstacles such as insufficient funding and, to a certain degree, lack of support among the regional actors. The Baltic countries themselves originally feared that this was yet another alternative to NATO membership, and were highly skeptical about the idea of economic cooperation with Russia, a country from which they were seeking independence, certainly not another form of control. The Nordic countries, for their part, had a great interest in creating bilateral commercial ties with the Baltic States, but supporting the US business community was not on the Nordic agenda.

Nevertheless, the NEI remained on the table. The *Baltic Charter*, signed by the Presidents of the three Baltic States and President Clinton at a ceremony in the White House on January 16, 1998, provided the next logical step in US strategy toward the region. Although the text only expressed a general state of friendship among the participating countries, the vigorous and reassuring language of the Charter underlined the American view that the Baltic States were an integral part of the US vision of the new Europe, and as entitled as anyone to join NATO at some point. The document was clearly an "indication of how much had changed since the end of the Cold War ... and of the promise of things to come," but also demonstrated that "some geopolitical verities remain unchanged," as Zakheim concludes.[197] According to the document, the United States "welcomes the aspirations and supports the efforts of Estonia, Latvia, and Lithuania to join NATO" once ready and able, and once NATO determines that "the inclusion of these nations would serve European stability and the strategic interests of the Alliance."[198] Aware of the strong opposition to the extension of NATO to former Soviet territory, the US and the Alliance cautiously avoided any wording that could be interpreted as referring to specific security guarantees, or a precise timetable in the Charter – a "date certain."[199]

Nevertheless, the document did provide a strong case that Baltic security had become a priority for the US. It confirmed that the Nordic-Baltic region had ascended in US strategy from its former position as strategic backwater to occupy a central role in American policy for Europe. That development had taken place in only a few years' time, and, some would argue, basically as a result of the active interest taken by only a handful of people at the top of the US Administration. Secretary of State Madeleine

---

197 Zakheim 1998, p. 115.

198 Charter of Partnership Among the United States of America and the Republic of Estonia, Republic of Latvia, and Republic of Lithuania," p. 4, also in *Baltic Sea Region Brief*, p. 111.

199 *The Economist*, January 17, 1998, Zakheim 1997, pp. 19 ff., Zakheim 1998, p. 116.

Albright had approached Baltic security as a critical test of the strength of the entire post-Cold War system, US strategy, and NATO enlargement in Europe. Under Secretary of State and Russia expert Strobe Talbott, although long an advocate for the "Russia first" strategy, claimed to have harbored an interest for the situation in the Baltic States ever since his years as a journalist stationed in Moscow, although this was rarely reflected in his policy recommendations. By the late 1990s, he had reportedly become an advocate for an open-door policy for the Baltic States, as long as such a policy was part of a broader framework, and combined with an effort to reach out to Moscow: "the Dual Track"[200]

5.2 The fourth phase: preparing a second round of enlargement (1999–2002)

5.2.1 A change of mood

In just a few years, there had been a dramatic change of mood in the downtown offices where the Nordic-Baltic issue is handled in Washington. Right up until the turn of the millennium, it was still far from certain whether the first round of NATO enlargement would be followed by a second wave – and in that case, whether all three Baltic States, or even any of them, would eventually be in the group admitted to membership the second time around.

A variety of factors may account for this pessimism. One obvious concern had to do with Russia: that enlargement to countries on the former Soviet territory could still prove much too provocative to Moscow. This was long the main (although mostly tacit) reason for delaying the process in Washington. A new era of bilateral contacts between the US and Russia also risked placing the Baltic countries and other small states at a distinct disadvantage as all other aspects of US policy were again rated second to its relations with Moscow. Many also saw Russia as already enjoying too much influence and insight in NATO as a result of the Founding Act, with Russian officials crowding the corridors of NATO HQ and at SHAPE – an arrangement with which the Baltic States were expressly unhappy. The creation of the new NATO–Russia Council in May 2002 renewed European concerns about US priorities, but was concluded only after the US had made clear that Moscow could not influence the American determination at this stage to include the Baltic countries in the rapidly expanding group of NATO countries. As this point had finally been reached, complaints

200 Asmus 2002, pp. 99 ff.

could be heard from both sides of the Atlantic (although not from the regional actors) that a "new NATO" with such a broad and heterogeneous membership would cease to function as a defense alliance, and become nothing but a second OSCE in character, membership and efficiency.

Domestic affairs have been cited as one of the most important reasons behind the shift in US policy from a rather remote attitude in the early and mid-1990s, seeking to divert the attention of the aspiring candidates by the creation of the PfP in 1994, to fully embracing the idea of an enlargement of NATO to the three Visigrad countries at the Madrid Summit in 1997, and with actual enlargement first taking place at the Washington Summit in April, 1999. If entry into the Alliance depended on the ethnicity of the American people, analysts wondered prior to the Prague Summit in 2002 with a second round rapidly approaching, would the three Baltic countries be able to gather the votes in a second round? Would the Baltic lobby be sufficiently strong – as the Polish had been, including also Hungary and the Czech Republic as members?

It was also questioned whether the US would in fact remain interested in the enlargement process, or turn to other issues, once a successful first wave of new members was concluded. There was wide debate about whether a second round would be easier to accomplish, assuming that the first round had been the main and decisive step, or whether a second round might be the more complicated one. The second round did not attract the historic drama that surrounded, and in different ways both facilitated and complicated, the first one; also, it was clear that the three Baltic candidates were not yet militarily ready in spite of all the efforts of their Nordic neighbors to enhance their militaries (and the slow preparations by the new members of the first round certainly did not strengthen the Baltic case). Furthermore, Russian opposition seemed even more vigorous the second time around, with enlargement on the former Soviet territory being contemplated. In addition, there was transatlantic disagreement within the Alliance on the procedure, while other issues such as the NMD and the ESDP had a tendency to dominate the agenda and occasionally take the focus away from enlargement. Early in the Bush Administration there was widespread speculation in Washington on a possible trade-off with Moscow, trading Baltic membership for Russian acceptance of the National Missile Defense plan.[201]

The question of whether another round would actually happen was settled when the date for the next NATO Summit was set for the fall of 2002; Prague, the capital of one of the new members, was picked as the

---

201 Larrabee 2001, pp. 2–3.

location; and the next step of enlargement was put on the agenda for the meeting. An invitation to join NATO was delivered to the seven countries formally selected by the Summit, and actual enlargement was expected to take place a year or two later, when the ratification process had been concluded by all parliaments.

But the outcome of this debate with regard to the Baltic countries remained highly uncertain up until almost the last minute. The positive formulations in the Baltic Charter, declaring that the goal shared by the US and its Baltic partners is "the full integration of Estonia, Latvia, and Lithuania into European and transatlantic political, economic, *security and defense institutions*" was not a vision subscribed to by all allied countries, nor for that matter by all analysts or even within the entire Clinton Administration in office at the time.[202] National Security Adviser Sandy Berger and others in his office had, for instance, warned against any formulations that could be seen to provide even a semi-security guarantee to the Baltic countries.[203]

While for some time only Denmark, and gradually the US, supported the idea of Baltic membership in NATO, in the end the idea also received strong support from Hungary, Poland, and Spain and with previously tepid Norway slowly warming to the concept. But Baltic inclusion in NATO encountered rather strong opposition from a number of significant European allies. Prominent in the group of skeptics was Germany, which after years of successfully advocating Polish membership – and thereby reaching its main goal, the stabilization of Central Europe, and the removal of the eastern border of NATO away from German territory – continued to fear a strong Russian reaction with regard to enlargement in the Baltic region.[204] The UK and Italy were also among the critics of such a development, only gradually accepting the idea of the Baltic countries as fellow members in NATO.[205]

Instead of a second round that would include the Baltic States among the new allies, some skeptics saw the EU, with an emerging ESDP slowly in the making, as the most natural affiliation for the three small states in the near future. This reasoning was based on the assumption that the EU, which more than a decade after the collapse of the Cold War still had not enlarged its membership to the former East bloc countries (though

---

202 "A Charter of Partnership." p. 3 (emphasis added).
203 Asmus 2002 presents an inside account of the issue of NATO enlargement in US policy, including to the Baltic countries, pp. 228 ff.
204 Larrabee 2001, p. 2.
205 Smith 2002, pp. 42 ff.

Sweden, Finland, and Austria were brought in as members in 1995), would eventually do so a couple of years into the new millennium. But as representatives of the three Baltic States were apt to point out, while the EU certainly enhances the security of its member states, it would not be capable of providing a realistic alternative to NATO membership, with or without a defense capacity of its own. In addition, Estonia was for long the only Baltic country more or less guaranteed membership as the Union enlarged, potentially leaving Lithuania and Latvia behind. With Lithuania long considered the frontrunner for NATO membership, such a scenario – favored by, among others, former National Security Adviser Zbigniew Brzezinski – would have been a solution that risked placing Latvia, with a large Russian population, in a potentially troublesome situation outside of both organizations.

5.2.2 The two nonaligned Nordic countries

An alternative solution to the regional security dilemma that was repeatedly mentioned during the enlargement debate was a "Max Jakobson" option of early Swedish and Finnish membership in NATO. As previously mentioned, such a scenario would enable the former neutral countries to take active responsibility for their vulnerable neighbors from positions within the Alliance, similar to the roles played by Denmark and Norway during the Cold War with regard to the nonaligned Nordic countries, Sweden in particular. But would Swedish–Finnish entrance into NATO prove less sensitive for Russia than Baltic membership? Or could it actually be seen as to Russia's advantage to have two countries familiar with the former superpower and, at least in the Swedish case, with a tendency to display a certain understanding of Russian sensitivities, inside NATO? Whatever the response, such a Nordic role seemed heavily reduced with the 2002 NATO–Russian agreement.

Over the years, it has been pointed out by NATO officials that Finland and Sweden would be welcome to join the Alliance whenever they wish.[206] Only in one respect, local experts point out, do they fail to qualify: in the low level of public support in their respective countries, crucial, since one precondition for NATO membership is that such a policy enjoys the support of the population. After a historic dip in the late 1990s when only 11 per cent of Finns were said to be in favor of NATO membership for their country, the numbers stabilized at around 20–25 per cent for years. In the spring of 2007 NATO support in Finland reached a high of 27 per

---

206 The most recent reference appeared in *The Economist*, June 30th–July 6th 2007.

cent in a survey conducted by *Turun Sanomat*.[207] Swedish polls have regularly reported around 30–35 per cent in favor, except in 1997 when Gallup showed a slim majority in favor of membership – quickly lost as numbers again dropped with the Kosovo campaign. A slow increase has, however, been noticed in the category of undecided, indicating a possible movement toward increased support of NATO.[208]

But while NATO HQ regularly issues informal invitations, mid-level regional officials at the State Department and diplomats at the Stockholm embassy have paradoxically often gone out of their way to assure the Swedish government of the many merits of nonalignment. Such statements by NATO's largest ally and the founder of the Alliance may seem puzzling, but were much appreciated by the Social Democratic governments of Sweden – the main architects and defenders of nonalignment – over the years.[209] The logical consequence of those statements (which have been contradicted by private remarks by US officials) would thus be that the US, or at least parts of the American Administration, supported NATO membership for the Baltic countries, but not for Sweden.

Unlike the many candidates that lined up to join NATO, the two Nordic countries are definitely militarily able, but not yet politically prepared to trade in their current security doctrines for membership in NATO. But as their Baltic neighbors moved to take up their positions as new members of NATO, the two nonaligned Nordic countries were confronted with an entirely new reality in their security environment, with possible consequences for themselves. Debate on the future security doctrine was steadily growing in Finland, where the government *Defense Review* presented in 2004 was assumed to suggest fundamental changes, quite possibly a recommendation for Finland to seek NATO membership. In the end, this did not materialize due to strong political opposition to such a move.[210] Sweden – with a more nostalgic attachment to the concepts of neutrality and nonalignment – has had little if any debate on the issue and noticeably little governmental interest for an altered security doctrine. (So far, this is true also for the new Non-Socialist government, which came to office in 2006, with Carl Bildt as Foreign Minister.) Over the years it has often been suggested that a Finnish application for NATO membership may be

---

207 *Turun Sanomat*, May 16, 2007.

208 For an overview of the NATO polls and Swedish–NATO relations generally, see Dahl 1999a.

209 Such statements have been made on a number of occasions; during various conversations with American diplomats in Stockholm over the past couple of years.

210 *Finlands säkerhets- och försvarspolitik 2004*, Ries 2001, 218. A new White Book will be presented in 2008.

the only scenario that could propel Sweden into action.[211] The next logical question would be which scenario could possibly provoke Finland into first making such a move, apart from an openly aggressive Russia.

Regardless of the state of the NATO debate at home, the two nonaligned Nordic countries steadily continued their efforts to improve the Baltic military preparedness in the new millennium, assistance that had continued since the early 1990s. Finland and Sweden were in part pursuing this policy on behalf of NATO and the US, as these actors could not themselves run the risk of appearing provocative toward Russia. The heavy investment by all Nordic countries to improve Baltic military structures and capabilities was made with the explicit objective of facilitating the Baltic countries' inclusion into NATO from a military (and civil-military) perspective, thus removing one potential obstacle from the agenda. The two nonaligned Nordic countries have thus been actively pursuing NATO membership for the three Baltic countries, while simultaneously rejecting such a course for themselves.

5.2.3   Bush II and the Baltic issue

As we have seen, only a handful of people were specifically assigned to deal with developments in the Baltic Sea region during the Clinton years. By consistently advocating an active American role, and by turning to the Nordic countries for ideas and advice, as well as for the practical implementation of this strategy, this group helped change the direction of US policy in the region.[212] It was initially uncertain whether the new Republican Administration, which took office in January 2001, would offer a similar kind of commitment to the Baltic cause.[213] But advocates of Baltic membership quickly felt encouraged by the talk given by the-then chairman of the Senate Foreign Relations Committee, Republican Jesse Helms at the American Enterprise Institute in January 2001. After he had first been given a more traditional speech, Helms tore out a couple of pages on the very morning of his presentation and turned the argument into basically a moral one. He declared:

> Perhaps the greatest moral challenge we face at the dawn of a new century is to right the wrongs perpetrated in the last century at Yalta, when the West abandoned the nations of Central and Eastern Europe to Stalin and a life of servitude behind the Iron Curtain.

---

211 See for instance op-ed arguing along this lines in *Hufvudstadsbladet*, February 6, 2002.
212 For an inside account of this process, see Asmus 2002.
213 Ibid, p. 305.

Helms went on to state his position with regards to the Baltic countries' aspirations to become members of NATO:

> I intend to work with the Bush Administration to ensure that the Baltic States are invited to join their neighbors Poland, Hungary and the Czech Republic, as members of the NATO alliance. This is vital not only for their security, but for ours as well. If we want good relations with Russia, we must show Russia's leaders an open path to good relations, while at the same time closing off their avenues to destructive behavior. That means taking the next step in the process of NATO expansion, by issuing invitations to the Baltic nations when NATO's leaders meet for the next alliance Summit planned for 2002.[214]

Baltic independence, Helms firmly stated, must not be a "temporary phenomenon," as it was apparently seen by some in Moscow.[215]

To those who had boldly argued the merits of a major "big bang" which would dramatically enlarge NATO to a majority of the candidate countries, Senator Helms' statement was encouraging. It expressed an idealist sentiment that Baltic membership was "the right thing to do," given the long suffering of the peoples of these countries and attaching a strong moral issue to their cause. The Baltic countries were seen as very much "like us" in Washington, DC – as Westernized societies and people with values and sentiments much like those held by the American people, further facilitating the understanding of their case and their entry into the Alliance.

Two events were crucial in shaping the enlargement policies of the Republican Administration. George W. Bush's trip to Europe in June, 2001, the first as president and the second ever for Mr. Bush, provided ample opportunities for Europeans and Americans to discuss the many items on the transatlantic agenda in the new millennium. For Sweden, President Bush's stop in Göteborg on June 14 was also a first: the first visit ever to Sweden by an American president in office. But celebrations in Sweden were muted by the anti-free trade demonstrations surrounding the meeting, and by the realization that the visit primarily was a result of the EU presidency which nonaligned Sweden happened to hold in the first six months of the year, and which coincided with the new president's trip overseas.

The president's stop in Warsaw on the same tour produced happier memories for everybody involved. Mr. Bush used the occasion to turn his speech at the University Library into a broad statement on his views

---

214 Address by Senator Jesse Helms at the American Enterprise Institute, January 11, 2001, pp. 5–6.
215 Ibid.

on the enlargement of NATO and his vision for Europe. The President declared:

> All of Europe's new democracies, from the Baltic to the Black Sea and all that lie between should have the same chance for security and freedom and the same chance to join the institutions of Europe as Europe's old democracies have. I believe in NATO membership for all of Europe's democracies that seek it and are ready to share the responsibility that NATO brings. The question of 'when' may be still up for debate within NATO; the question of 'whether' should not be.

And the President added:

> As we plan the Prague Summit, we should not calculate how little we can get away with, but how much we can do to advance the cause of freedom. The expansion of NATO has fulfilled NATO's promise, and that promise now leads eastward and southward, northward and onward.[216]

Three months later, the terrorist attacks against the World Trade Center and the Pentagon dramatically altered the entire agenda for the Western world. The main issue now was the war on terrorism; the new American priorities were expressed in the President's order to his staff to make sure quite simply to "finish the job" on enlargement – including in the Baltic region – and not let it get in the way of the main task being pursued.

For Russia, aspiring to a place in the Western world, opposition to enlargement of NATO to the former Soviet territory had not diminished either in principle or in the official line emanating from certain parts of Moscow. In practice, however, Baltic membership in NATO was now seen as a lost cause for Russia that could only result in a loss of prestige for both Putin and his country if it remained on the agenda. And it was definitely not worth risking the new partnership that President Putin had established with his American counterpart in the new world that emerged from the ashes of Ground Zero, New York City.

---

[216] "Remarks by President George W. Bush at University Library, Warsaw, Poland, 16 June, 2001."

5.3 The fifth phase: a new security system in the Nordic-Baltic region (2002–2007)

Following the invitation issued at the Prague Summit in 2002 to start membership negotiations with NATO, the three former Soviet republics officially joined NATO in 2004 and the EU – which carried out a similar "big bang" when enlarging its membership to 27 countries on the European continent. The global war on terror has kept the superpower fully occupied in the Middle East, but with the Baltic countries firmly anchored in the Western security structures, and with all regional countries except Sweden and Finland members of NATO, there was no longer any doubt about the US commitment to security in the Nordic-Baltic region. It's clear that "NATO expansion is the best way to keep Washington focused on the area".[217] The same would undoubtedly be the case for the two remaining nonaligned Nordic countries, Finland and Sweden.

The Baltic membership in NATO removed the gray zone dilemma once and for all, securing the region in the West and providing a much-needed protection for the three small countries from any revanchist ambitions that may still be harbored in Moscow. Under President Putin, Russia still has difficulty accepting the fact that the former Soviet republics are now fully sovereign and independent states, as shown by regular imperialist outbursts such as during the Estonian "statue conflict" in the spring of 2007. Increased Russian use of energy supply as the principal foreign policy instrument, and announcements that the navy will defend the gas pipeline jointly planned with Germany to run through the Baltic Sea, suggest the return of the Baltic Sea, the Barents area (with substantial energy resources), and the Northern region in general on the international security agenda. Bilateral agreements in the field of energy cooperation were signed in the summer of 2007 between the US and Sweden and Denmark, respectively.[218] During the same period, Russia also warned of a possible military escalation in the enclave of Kalingrad on the Baltic Sea coast in response to US plans for a missile defense system in Poland and the Czech Republic.[219]

The Baltic countries have enjoyed an enormous surge in security since their formal admission into NATO in 2004. Their membership in the Alliance also resulted in some unexpected bonuses for the three small countries, which now take turns serving as NATO contact points for their

217 Dörfer 1997, p. 94–95.
218 With Denmark, on June 26 and 27, 2007, and with Sweden, on June 28, 2007.
219 *Berlingske Tidende*, July 6, 2007.

larger, nonaligned neighbors, Finland and Sweden. As the PfP experienced a drastic drain of partner countries with the "big bang" in 2004, the two Nordic nonaligned countries found themselves in an odd and disparate group consisting of "the stans" and a small handful of former neutral countries, with little very in common. As a result of this curious arrangement, both the two Nordic countries and NATO started looking for other venues for meaningful cooperation.

To balance their position as non-members of NATO, both countries have made heavy investments in the Nordic Battle Group set up by the European Union. The four participating countries reflect the new forms of cooperation: nonaligned EU members Sweden and Finland, NATO and EU member Estonia, and Norway, a NATO but non-EU country which sees the Battle Group as a way to compensate for the political and military marginalization which it has experienced in the post-Cold War era. Sweden has taken the lead in the Battle Group, and has also intensified its bilateral cooperation with NATO ally Norway, particularly in surveillance and intelligence-sharing, to complement the close military contacts the country already enjoys with fellow nonaligned Finland (dating back to World War I).[220] In addition, both have – in spite of not being formal members of NATO – received invitations to participate in the Response Force set up by NATO (the NRF), where Denmark in particular is already making a large contribution. All Nordic and Baltic countries have troops in NATO's mission in Afghanistan, ISAF, while Denmark is also part of the US-led Coalition of the Willing (until August, 2007) in Iraq.

---

220 Dörfer 1997, p. 87.

6. The Nordic-Baltic Region and the Unipolar Values

6.1 Nordic bandwagoning and "Europeanization"

While the geopolitical and strategic relationship shows a gradually mounting unipolar interest in the Northern part of the European continent, the political pattern comes across as much less complex during the unipolar period. The unipolar victory resulted in a clear ideological and political movement of the Nordic region in a westward direction. The Nordic interest in the strategic destiny of the Baltic countries was matched by homogeneous political tendencies on both sides of the Baltic Sea, which were further enhanced by extensive Nordic programs of assistance to strengthen Baltic democracy and market economy. Apart from the enthusiasm displayed by the Baltic countries during their campaigns for NATO membership (and to a much lesser extent membership in the EU, with NATO as their # 1 priority), the consequences of this ideological movement were particularly evident in nonaligned Finland and Sweden in the early 1990s. The successful conclusion of the first Gulf War, which temporarily silenced the traditional anti-American voices critical not only of that war but of the US generally, coincided with the Swedish election later the same year of the first government headed by a Conservative prime minister – and, in addition, one who was overtly pro-American – since the 1930s. But NATO membership was not on the agenda of the new government in Sweden (and was also not on the official program for the next Non-Socialist government headed by Fredrik Reinfeldt which won the parliamentary election in 2006). Meanwhile in Finland, an application to the first round of NATO enlargement was expected by many during the joint tenure of President Ahtisaari and Prime Minister Lipponen, but stalled due to political obstacles.[221]

The political shift was not limited only to the nonaligned part of the Nordic region in the first period of the unipolar years. Similar movements could be seen also in NATO countries Denmark, Iceland, and Norway. The general trend in favor of unipolar values resulted in a strong tendency among all Nordic countries to *bandwagon* (or engage in anti-balance-of-power behavior) with the sole remaining superpower.[222] Rather than follow the theoretical assumptions of political science theorists, arguing that smaller actors almost reflexively balance against the hegemonic power, the strong tendency to side with the winner of the Cold War made the geopolitical as well as political-ideological imbalance in its favor even greater. From a group of previously hesitant and critical allies (Denmark, Norway, and Iceland), a silent partner (Sweden), and a Soviet neighbor that had had neutrality imposed on it by geopolitical circumstances (Finland) during the Cold War, the Nordic countries made a decisive westward political turn in the early 1990s.

This was quite a change from previous years – "[i]t is a far cry from the days, not too long ago, when Pentagon officials regarded Denmark more as an irritant than as an ally within the councils of NATO," noted one former US official.[223] For its part, Norway harbored a great fear after the end of the Cold War that the mental and material reduction of American interest, equipment, and involvement in Europe would leave Norway unprotected in the North; thus, the brief returning interest in Oslo for a European connection through the EU and WEU. After a decade when superpower attention on the Nordic region had primarily been concentrated on the Northern Flank and Norway, the country experienced an unaccustomed sense of neglect as unipolarity moved the focus instead to the Baltic Sea region. Norway also dealt with the new strategic situation by increasingly turning to the use and advocacy of soft power instruments.[224]

In the first years of unipolarity, this Nordic policy of bandwagoning with the West was mainly performed through a determined strategy of *Europeanization*. For Sweden, Finland, and Norway, all of whom handed in their application forms for membership to the then-EC in 1991, this

---

221 Ries 2001, p. 216.
222 For studies on bandwagoning, especially in the Nordic countries, see Mouritzen 1991 and 1992, and Dahl 1997a.
223 Zakheim 1997, p. 21.
224 Thune and Ulriksen 2002, Dörfer 1997, pp. 36 ff.

strategy was embarked upon in an effort to adapt their societies to the requirements presented by the European Community (from 1995 renamed the European Union). By the time the rounds of referenda had been concluded at the end of 1994, the enthusiastic public support which had been noted in the earlier stages of the campaign had all but faded in Sweden (where the vote in favor of EC/EU membership had only a slim majority), while the Norwegian electorate once again opted out of the joint European venture. To many Norwegians, the word "Union" provoked historic memories of the union shared until 1905 with their neighbor Sweden, an experience they apparently were not eager to repeat. Only in Finland, more immediately concerned than the other two about keeping the historic "window of opportunity" open, did the strong public support for the EC/EU survive the referendum.

Sweden continued to top the statistics as the country with the most EU-negative population of all member states for a few years into the millennium. While Finland traded in her Finnish marks for the euro on January 1, 2002, Sweden and Denmark joined the United Kingdom in opting out of first-round participation in the EMU. Both the subsequent Swedish referendum on the monetary union in the fall of 2002, and the Danish vote on the EU Constitution the following year, were rejected by narrow majorities.

6.2 The transatlantic link

The diminishing interest in the European cause was to some extent compensated for by an intensified pattern of transatlantic cooperation. This was particularly true for the countries outside the Alliance. Nonaligned Finland and Sweden had both, for practical purposes, abandoned "neutrality" as a concept when entering the European Union. In the Swedish case "neutrality" was however still maintained in official rhetoric, with neutrality part of its security doctrine until 2002. At that point, the traditional doctrine was finally modified and neutrality described as a doctrine that "had served Sweden well in the past." As a result of its EU membership, Finland declared itself to be nonaligned "under current circumstances" – which, however, kept changing.

The two nonaligned Nordic countries quickly turned out to be committed and enthusiastic participants in the NATO-sponsored Partnership for Peace program (jointly with the Baltic countries, which however saw the PfP as a stepping-stone to NATO membership) and the EAPC from day one, and were among the very first to sign up in 1994. Both countries have prided themselves on their unique role in the program as security *producers* rather than the much more extensive group of *consumers*. In preparation for the dramatic downsizing of the PfP group that was predicted to happen after the second round of NATO enlargement, Sweden and Finland produced a joint proposal, discussing ways to maintain the PfP as a relevant instrument.[225] Regardless of the ideological character of their respective governments, Finland and Sweden have thus proven to be staunch supporters of the transatlantic link in the post-Cold War world. As we have seen, in the Swedish case the tight cooperation with the US and a number of NATO countries actually dated back to the late 1940s, as documented by two officially appointed commissions in 1994 and 2002.

But while the conclusions of the two reports were nothing short of astounding for a country and government that had proudly proclaimed its nonaligned and neutral status all through the Cold War era, the public reaction was surprisingly rather lukewarm. Lingering affection for what is still, in spite of the widely reported conclusions presented by the Commissions, seen as an independent line of policy in the Cold War, remains evident in the formerly neutral, now nonaligned country. In a similar way, anti-Americanism did not vanish with the Cold War in the Nordic (or European) countries, just because their governments started emphasizing the significance of the transatlantic link. Rather, anti-Americanism seemed actually to have made something of a comeback as a political trend at the end of the 1990s, when the campaign in Kosovo produced a dramatic drop in public support of NATO in the Nordic countries, as well as in many other parts of Europe. The decision by the Bush Administration and the "Coalition of the Willing" to go to war in Iraq in 2003 further strengthened the anti-American tendency.

It was commonly emphasized on both sides of the Atlantic that relations between the US and the Nordic countries had never been as good or as close as was the case in the mid-1990s – only with the later exception of the fall of 2001.[226] Finland, which had been involuntarily dependent on the Soviet Union throughout the Cold War as a result of the pact on mutual friendship and cooperation, and enjoyed a heroic image in the US after fighting several wars against the giant, was now referred to as the de facto "17th member" of and by the Alliance.[227] This description had previ-

---

225 See Järvenpää 2003a, pp. 110 ff.
226 Speech by US Ambassador to Copenhagen, Ambassador Edward Elson in Malmö in December 1997.
227 Conversation with Ron Asmus: also see Asmus 1997b, p. 41.

ously been applied to Sweden through the duration of the Cold War and during the Bildt government of 1991–1994.

It was no coincidence that Finland replaced Sweden in that category. After the mid-1990s, Sweden was often seen in the US as too absorbed in nostalgia for neutrality, especially during Ingvar Carlsson's second tenure as Prime Minister (1994–1996), when attempts were made to return to more traditional interpretations of neutrality. His successor, fellow Social Democrat Göran Persson, lacked any experience in foreign policy before taking up the post, but quickly established an image for himself as a, relatively speaking, pro-American – even pro-Israeli – force in the Swedish government, sometimes producing a split with more ideological parts of the Social Democratic party (among them the late Foreign Minister Anna Lindh) in the process. On the question of NATO, both Persson and Lindh were adamant in declaring that Sweden, in the Prime Minister's words, "will never join NATO" – often with reference to the restraining effect that a change of doctrine would presumably have on any ambitions to pursue an activist foreign policy.[228] On the opposite side of the Bothnia, the election of Finnish President Tarja Halonen in 2000 was a serious setback to the pro-NATO forces in Finland, but after more than a year of silence, the issue of NATO slowly began making its way back on the agenda, gently pushed by some members of government, in preparation for the 2004 Defense Review.[229] Halonen's reelection in 2006 however further delayed the issue of NATO membership for Finland.

During the 1990s, much Nordic policy was thus geared toward meeting American approval and support, a far cry from the distancing that had characterized the official approach to the transatlantic link in earlier, Cold War years. This novel Nordic ambition to openly adopt the role of a transatlantic team player was evident not only in the Baltic Sea, but also very clearly in Bosnia and Kosovo where the former neutrals performed under NATO command in IFOR, SFOR, and KFOR, and also for Denmark and Norway during the repeated crises in the 1990s between Iraq and the US, later to erupt into full-scale war.[230] Acknowledging the significance and

---

228 The activist policies of several NATO countries, such as Canada, Denmark, Norway and the Netherlands, contradict this conclusion. See Dahl & Hillmer, 2002a for a comparative study of the activist foreign policies of NATO and nonaligned countries.

229 The Defense Review is discussed by Ries 2001; for the report, see *Finlands Säkerhets- och försvarspolitik 2004*.

230 For example, in the US–Iraq conflict in the winter of 1998, Denmark and Norway declared their willingness to participate with for instance aircraft, though soldiers would not be dispatched. A staunch believer in the UN, the (Social Democratic) government of Sweden insisted in 1991 as well as in 1998 and 2003 on the need to find a diplomatic solution.

scope of the unipolar power, the Nordic countries were making every effort not to provoke the Americans politically in the last decade of the old millennium, as had previously been the usual pattern during bipolarity. Instead, the Nordic countries went out of the way to work *with* the Americans in every possible way and area.

6.3   September 11, 2001 – and Iraq, 2003

The strong tendency to side – or "bandwagon" – with the US further escalated as a result of the tragic events of September 11, 2001. The Nordic countries and, more predictably, the Baltic countries, stepped forward determinedly as strong supporters of the US, sharply condemning the terrorists responsible for the horrendous acts, and proclaiming the attacks against the World Trade Center and the Pentagon as attacks on them all, as part of the Western world, and on its values and lifestyle. The EU Summit Declaration issued shortly after the attack was signed by the three Nordic members, and complemented by separate statements issued by the respective governments. A number of programs for military, economic, humanitarian, intelligence, and other forms of assistance to fight Islamist terrorism, including within the *Operation Enduring Freedom*, were elaborated in close contact with US authorities. Norway, Denmark, and Iceland expressed their solidarity with the stricken superpower when NATO collectively activated the Washington Treaty's Article Five, for the first time in the history of the Alliance.

The Nordic expressions of solidarity with the US were delivered irrespective of the ideological leaning of the various governments. In the Swedish parliament, Prime Minister Göran Persson declared, with a formulation borrowed from his French colleagues that in times like that, "we are all Americans." This statement of expressed solidarity with the United States was in many ways unique.[231] After all, this was a country that was once blacklisted by Washington for its vociferous criticism of American foreign policy, and a Social Democratic government that in previous decades had often made anti-Americanism a centerpiece of its rhetoric when attempting to portray itself as a "moral superpower" in international affairs.[232] The statement was particularly interesting given the difficulties in transatlantic understanding that have traditionally characterized

---

231 Sweden in the unipolar years is discussed in Dahl 2006b, an early analysis is found in Dahl 1997a.

232 For a study of Swedish activism in the Cold War era, see Nilsson (Dahl) 1991a.

relations between European Socialist parties and Republican administrations in Washington. But this turned out to be a brief historic moment in Swedish politics: the strong pro-American line was soon abandoned as Sweden became the only European country not only consistently to voice criticism of the Guantánamo camp, but also to actively demand the release of a citizen held prisoner in the camp.[233]

Persson's colleague to the south, Liberal Danish Prime Minister Anders Fogh Rasmussen, traveled to Washington on several occasions after the September events. On a visit to George Washington University in March 2002, where the Danish Prime Minister received an honorary doctorate, Fogh Rasmussen declared that:

> Our shared values point Europe and North America towards a common destiny. ... We must – and do – depend on each other. We have no choice but to act in concert in our unpredictable and sometimes dangerous world.[234]

But while Fogh Rasmussen enthusiastically announced that relations between Denmark and the US had never been in better shape, the Conservative government in Norway came forward as another early opponent of the American treatment of the al-Qaida prisoners at the Guantánamo camp in Cuba. Long-standing Norwegian ambitions to serve as a mediator in the Middle East, with frequent Norwegian complaints about the US approach toward the Palestinian problem, may have influenced the Norwegian stand in this regard.[235] A more low-key response to the entire post-September 11 situation was presented by Finland's government – lukewarm at best, critics said, complaining that this might have given the impression of less than wholehearted Finnish support to the coalition against terrorism. The unenthusiastic government response to an American request in September, 2002 for flights over Finnish territory contributed to raising some questions concerning the country's commitment to the anti-terrorist cause.[236]

The prelude to the US-led operation in Iraq in 2003, and the war itself, demonstrated the deep division that had developed within a few years among the Nordic-Baltic actors with regard to US policy.[237] Of a grand total of 15 European countries, Denmark was the only Nordic country to

---

233 Mouritzen 2004, p. 31.
234 "Lecture by Prime Minister Anders Fogh Rasmussen, The George Washington University, Wednesday, 27th of March, 2002."
235 *Economist*, May 25th, 2002.
236 Ries 2001, p. 223 f.
237 Mouritzen 2004, pp. 22 ff.

participate with military troops in the *Coalition of the Willing* led by the US. In addition, Denmark remained in Iraq several years longer than most of the countries in the Coalition, and only left Iraq as late as August, 2007, when the force was transferred to join the Danish troops already on the ground in the violent Helmand province in the south of Afghanistan. With this record Denmark comes across as one of the most loyal European allies to the United States in Iraq (as was also the case in Afghanistan).

As one of the charter members of the Alliance, Denmark was indeed an old NATO ally, but the country nevertheless clearly belonged in the category of "new Europe," to use the phrase coined by Defense Secretary Rumsfeld. Denmark signed the open letter, which was published in support of the United States in early 2003. So did the three Baltic countries, which by all standards belonged in the "new Europe," consisting mostly of former Warsaw Bloc countries, that rarely hesitated to provide assistance to the US in the war on terror. Iceland, which was at the time confronted with the final withdrawal of US troops and imminent US plans to close the Keflavik base (a move which Iceland itself had proposed several times in the past but now firmly opposed), also provided diplomatic support to the US.

On the other side of the diplomatic battlefield were Norway, Finland, and Sweden, all of whom were traditional, solid supporters of the UN and which all now came across as firm opponents to the US-led operation in Iraq. In fact, of all the European countries, Sweden is described by Hans Mouritzen as one of the two most anti-American at this time, jointly with Belgium, due to the intense legal campaign against US authorities to release its citizen in the Guantánamo camp.[238] Given the record of anti-American rhetoric which characterized Sweden during the Cold War, the position with regard to *Operation Iraqi Freedom* definitely seems more in line with traditional Swedish diplomacy than the unique – and politically and personally courageous – support that had been given to the NATO bombings in Kosovo in 1999 by the then-Foreign Minister Anna Lindh.[239]

Swedish foreign policy took yet another turn with the arrival of the Non-Socialist Reinfeldt government in 2006. The new, and openly pro-American Prime Minister, paid an official visit to President Bush in the Oval Office only months after the election victory; the meeting was clearly facilitated by the similarities in ideological backgrounds of the two leaders. The PM came out of the meeting full of praise for the American President. The discussion mainly centered on environmental issues, with

---

238 Mouritzen 2004, p. 32.
239 Dahl 2006b, p. 904 ff.

the PM hoping to persuade the President to modify his position on the Kyoto Protocol – the war in Iraq or foreign policy more broadly was not on the agenda.[240]

In Finland, the new government coming to power after the March 2007 elections and including a strong representation from the Conservative Party (Kokoomus), took a clear step towards the United States by openly declaring in its Government program that it will seek improvement in Finnish–US Relations. A sign confirming this new policy direction was a visit by the new Foreign Minister, Ilkka Kanerva, to Washington to meet with his American counterpart, Condoleezza Rice in June 2007. There was lots of symbolism attached to that visit, since it had been an open secret in Helsinki political circles that the US administration did not extend invitations to Kanerva's predecessor, Erkki Tuomioja, or for that matter, to Tarja Halonen, the President of the Republic. The close new relationship between the US and Finland was again confirmed during the September 2007 visit by the Finnish Defense Minister, Jyri Häkämies, to Washington, where he gave a much-cited talk at the Center for Strategic and International Relations, and received a warm welcome by top-level US officials.[241]

---

240 *Svenska Dagbladet*, May 14 and 15, 2007.
241 For Jyri Häkämies' talk at CSIS, see www.csis.org and www.defmin.fi.

7. Conclusion

7.1 The Nordic region in US strategy during bipolarity

The Cold War represented a period that was in many ways unique, not just because of its exceptionally long duration of almost half a century. Of equal historic importance was the complete divisiveness of this historic period, splitting the world politically and militarily in two parts, with only a handful of exceptions – exceptions which ultimately, however, often proved to have sided with one of the bipolar parties, as the secret Swedish cooperation with NATO exemplifies. Not only was the world ideologically divided into two parts, under the auspices of the two superpowers that each assembled a group of closely allied countries around them, but the two blocs were basically inaccessible to one another, further adding to the lack of understanding. The division of the world was complete, in both military and ideological terms. The military doctrine of Containment was a true reflection of the two areas upon which US national security has traditionally been based – combining concepts of geopolitics and military strategy with political values and an idealist ambition to better the world by supporting and encouraging pluralist democracy worldwide.

In this global scheme to contain the enemy, the Nordic region emerged as of particular value to the US when the Cold War had a strong bipolar character; when the ideological and military struggle was played out between two giant superpowers rather than two blocs or alliances. While the Central Front remained the strategic focus for NATO (and the Warsaw Pact) throughout the period, the American perspective tended to stretch farther north, thereby granting the Northern Flank and the Atlantic Islands greater strategic value and significance than was the case in Alliance policy.

For the US, it was the proximity to the superpower adversary, not the Front that primarily mattered in this perspective. Thus, the increased strategic interest toward the Nordic region from the late 1970s on, when the reinforced Soviet Navy operating out of the Kola Peninsula (only a short distance from the Nordic region) was identified as posing a direct challenge to US interests. The short distance between US and Soviet territories strengthened the interest in the Arctic and the High North on both sides of the ideological dividing line, with the American Thule base on Greenland located exactly equidistant to the two bipolar capitals. In the early period of the Cold War, as the doctrine of massive retaliation was replaced by the protracted doctrine of flexible response, and a central element of uncertainty was introduced in US planning, the strategic vulnerability of the Nordic region was generally seen to have increased. During the 1970s the Nordic region – and Europe in general – was largely neglected, with a consequent sense of abandonment, as the US became submerged in problems both on the domestic front and the all-consuming war in Vietnam.

Generally speaking, it was only when strategic developments were seen as posing a more or less direct threat to US interests that the region, and its diverse subregions, became of direct interest to Washington. The strategic role that the region was granted in US security policy, and the fluctuating strategic interest that it managed to evoke among policy-makers and strategists on that side of the Atlantic, was a result of its geopolitical location directly between the two superpower adversaries engaged in bipolar competition. Tight bipolarity and sensitive superpower relations, and more aggressive behavior by the Soviet Union, had an obvious and positive effect on the amount of American interest for this geographically peripheral region.

While the Nordic position in the bilateral system was easy to identify from a military-strategic perspective – with a number of crucial subregions around the Baltic exits; on the vital path crossing the Atlantic; and next to Soviet territory in the High North – the role that the region played in ideological Containment was more difficult to assess. All five Nordic countries had an independent streak that at times complicated the global ideological struggle under US leadership. This reluctance to fully and openly side with the Americans while militarily dependent on the US and NATO – and with nonaligned Sweden which participated in the allied struggle as a secret "seventeenth member" (an arrangement of which the

Swedish population was not aware) – put a serious and unnecessary strain on the US–Nordic relationship during the Cold War. But even though Nordic participation from a US perspective was often less than wholehearted, both in ideological and military Containment, the importance of the region within the Western sphere was never doubted by the Americans – troop and base restrictions, nuclear weapons caveats, Danish footnotes on NATO policy, and Swedish attempts at free-riding notwithstanding.

7.2 The Nordic-Baltic region in US strategy in the post-Cold War era

As the bipolar period was succeeded by a unipolar world, the question of whether the US was ready to defend its unique position of preeminence by actively assuming the obligations of a global role, or whether unipolar hegemony could be combined with a more insular attitude to the outside world, was intensely debated in and outside Washington. European concerns that the US was preparing for a massive withdrawal from the Continent were fueled by its dismantling of large parts of its military presence overseas, while NATO implemented a series of changes in the command structure that separated the Scandinavian allies in different commands, and further increased Norwegian fears of isolation. However, the idea of enlarging NATO by accepting a number of Warsaw Pact countries into the Western security sphere took hold in the mid-1990s, as the critical situation on the Balkans finally managed to elicit American engagement. These were encouraging signs that the US was indeed committed to the role as a "European power," manifest in President Clinton's sweeping promises to a "Europe whole and free".

How then was American policy applied to the extended Nordic-Baltic region that emerged with the end of the Cold War? What role was the region granted in unipolar American strategy?

The unipolar period saw a strong ideological and political movement of the Nordic countries in a westward direction – and this was particularly true for the three Baltic countries, which regained their sovereignty after a generation in Soviet custody. This ideological movement may have created the impression that the US enjoyed a presence of unprecedented dimensions in the region. But, from a strategic perspective, the opposite picture emerged in the early years of unipolarity as, with the disappearance of the Soviet threat, Washington concluded that the situation in the Northern part of the continent was as peaceful and stable as Central and Eastern Europe had become. Academics witnessed a profound lack of American interest in the region which prevailed up until the mid-1990s, in spite of the negative impacts of the 1990 CFE Treaty on the Northern Flank and the fact that this remained a heavily militarized region, still located next door to the Kola Peninsula, the Leningrad Military District, and Kaliningrad, and with a high level of instability characterizing the situation in the newly independent Baltic states. Fierce Russian opposition to Baltic hopes for NATO membership – and the security guarantees that accompanied such membership – long had a paralyzing effect on US policy toward the Baltic Sea. Only gradually did Washington acknowledge that the Nordic-Baltic region was in fact one of the most critical strategic areas of Europe, with a huge potential impact on European and global security – and that this situation required US leadership, not avoidance of the problem.

With a more realistic American perception of the strategic situation in the North, the emergence of a new subregion was confirmed in US policy. The Cold War subregions were relegated to more obscure positions as the Central Front in Europe was erased and the strategic scene remodeled. Only the very northernmost part of Europe was still granted high-level attention, though undoubtedly secondary to the Baltic Sea region. US interest became almost exclusively focused on the new subregion in the Baltic Sea (uniting the Nordic and Baltic countries around the Sea). While both areas were officially referred to as political priorities, the Nordic-Baltic region ascended in the latter part of the 1990s to a central role in US strategy to "secure a peaceful, undivided, and democratic Europe," as Secretary of State Madeleine Albright and her associates often described the relationship.[242] Her ambassador to Sweden joined her in arguing that stability in the region posed a litmus test for the new European security architecture, declaring that "the United States has a real, profound and enduring interest in the independence, sovereignty, and territorial integrity and security of Estonia, Latvia and Lithuania."[243]

For tactical reasons, and out of concern for Russian sensitivities, much of the practical implementation of this policy was carried out by the Nordic countries, with the US itself staying on the sidelines, providing encouragement and "value-added."[244] The American reliance on its Nordic partners to implement much of their shared strategic visions resulted in a number of extensive Nordic programs to assist Baltic independence and facilitate their applications for NATO membership.

The entry of the three former Soviet republics into NATO in 2004

---

242 Asmus 1997b, p. 35.
243 Speech by Ambassador Olson, February 26, 1998.
244 For example, Asmus 1997b, p. 39.

marked the beginning of a brand-new security system in the region. Even though two countries remain formally nonaligned, institutionally all countries are now solidly incorporated into the Western political and defense structures and the bulk of the Nordic-Baltic countries enjoy solid US defense guarantees. Such guarantees might come in handy as Russia is again starting to assert itself on the foreign policy scene, using energy supply as its new instrument to impose its presence on the region, as well as on the global scene.

Bibliography

Graham Allison and Gregory F. Treverton (eds.), *Rethinking America's Security. Beyond Cold War to New World Order* (New York: W.W Norton & Company, 1992).

Clive Archer, "The North as a Multidimensional Strategic Arena," in Martin O. Heisler (ed.), *The Nordic Region: Changing Perspectives in International Relations* (The Annals of the American Academy of Political and Social Science, November 1990).

—, "Nordic Involvement in the Baltic States Security: Needs, Response and Success," European Security research programme, Working Paper 1997.

Ronald D. Asmus, "NATO Enlargement and Baltic Security," in Bo Huldt and Ulrika Johannessen (eds.), *1st Annual Stockholm Conference on Baltic Sea Security and Cooperation* (Stockholm: Swedish Institute of International Affairs 1997a).

—, "American Views in Security and Cooperation in the Baltic Sea Region," in Joseph Kruzich and Anna Fahraeus, *2nd Annual Stockholm Conference on Baltic Security and Co-operation. Towards an Inclusive Security Structure in the Baltic Sea Region* (Stockholm: US Embassy, 1997b).

—, *Opening NATOs Door. How the Alliance Remade Itself for a New Era* (New York: Columbia University Press, 2002).

Ronald D. Asmus, Richard L. Kugler and F. Stephen Larrabee, "Building a New NATO," *Foreign Affairs* Sept/Oct 1993.

—, "NATO Expansion: The Next Steps," *Survival*, No 1, Spring 1995.

Ronald D. Asmus and Robert C. Nurick, "NATO Enlargement and the Baltic States," *Survival*, Summer 1996.

John C. Ausland, *Nordic Security and the Great Powers* (Boulder, Colo: Westview Press, 1986).

Carl Bildt, "The Baltic Litmus Test," *Foreign Affairs* Sept/Oct, 1994.

—, "Skapa ett nordeuropeiskt partnerskap för fred," *Svensk Tidskrift*, No. 4, 1996.

Zbigniew Brzezinski, "A Geostrategy for Eurasia," *Foreign Affairs* Sept/Oct, 1997.

—, *The Geostrategic Triad. Living with China, Europe, and Russia.* (Washington, DC: The CSIS Press, 2001).

Zbigniew Brzezinski and F. Stephen Larrabee, *US Policy toward Northeastern Europe: Report of an Independent Task Force Sponsored by the Council on Foreign Relations* (New York: Council on Foreign Relations, 1999).

Arne Olav Brundtland, "Norwegian Security Policy: Defense and Nonprovocation in a Changing Context," in Gregory Flynn (ed.), *NATO's Northern Allies. The National Security Policies of Belgium, Denmark, the Netherlands, and Norway* (Totowa, New Jersey: Rowman & Allanheld, 1985).

Arne Olav Brundtland and Don M. Snider, *Nordic-Baltic Security. An International Perspective* (Washington, DC: CSIS, 1994).

Barry Buzan, *People, States, and Fear: An Agenda for International Security in the Post-Cold War Era* (New York: Harvester Wheatsheaf, 1991).

Jacob Børresen, Gullow Gjeseth and Rolf Tamnes, *Allianseforsvar i endring, 1970–2000* (Bergen: Norsk forsvarshistorie, bind 5. Eide forlag, 2004).

Stephen A. Cambone, *The Implications of US Foreign and Defence Policy for the Nordic/Baltic Region* (Washington, DC: CSIS, 1993).

Wilhelm M.Carlgren, *Swedish Foreign Policy During the Second World War* (London: Benn, 1977).

Paul M. Cole, *U.S Security Assistance to Non-NATO Countries: The Swedish Case and Post-Communist Eastern Europe* (Santa Monica: RAND, 1992)

Paul M. Cole, "Atomic Bombast: A Swedish Nuclear Weapon?" *The Washington Quarterly* (Vol. 20, No. 2, Spring 1997)

Ann-Sofie Dahl (Nilsson), *Den Moraliska Stormakten. En studie av socialdemokratins internationella aktivism.* (Stockholm: Timbro, 1991a).

—, "Swedish Social Democracy in Central America: The Politics of Small State Solidarity," in *Journal of Interamerican Studies*, Vol. 33, No. 3, Fall 1991b.

Ann-Sofie Dahl, "To Be or Not To Be Neutral: Swedish Security strategy in the Post-Cold War Era," in Efraim Inbar and Gabriel Scheffer (eds.), *The National Security of Small States in a Changing World* (London: Frank Cass, 1997a).

—, "Not if but how: Sweden's future relations with NATO", *NATO Review*, No. 3, May-June 1997b.

—, *Svenskarna och NATO* (Stockholm: Timbro, 1999a).

—, "Sweden and the Baltic Sea Region – Activism on a New Arena or the End of Free-riding?" in Olav F. Knudsen (ed.), *Stability and Security in the Baltic Sea Region* (London: Frank Cass Publishers, 1999b).

—, "Activist Sweden: The Last Defender of Non-Alignment," in Ann-Sofie Dahl and Norman Hillmer (eds.), *Activism and (non)alignment* (Stockholm: Swedish Institute for International Affairs, 2002b).

—, "Baltikum – moderaternas väg till NATO," in Torbjörn Nilsson (ed.), *Anfall eller försvar. Högern i svensk politik under 1900-talet* (Stockholm: Santérus, 2002c).

—, "Den transatlantiska gemenskapen post-Irak", in Bertel Heurlin and Sten Rynning (eds.), *Det 21. århundredes trusler* (Copenhagen: DIIS, 2006a).

—, "Once a Moral Superpower, Always a Moral Superpower?", *International Journal* (Ottawa), Autumn, 2006b.

Ann-Sofie Dahl and Norman Hillmer (eds.), *Activism and (non)alignment* (Stockholm: Swedish Institute for International Affairs, 2002a).
Robert Dalsjö, *Life-Line Lost* (Stockholm: Santérus Academic Press Sweden, 2006).
Ingemar Dörfer, "Scandinavia and NATO: à la carte", *The Washington Quarterly*, Winter 1986.
—, *Nollpunkten. Sverige i det andra kalla kriget* (Stockholm: Timbro, 1991).
—, *The Nordic Nations in the New Security Regime* (Washington, DC: The Woodrow Wilson Center, 1997).
—, *America's Grand Strategy. Implications for Sweden.* (Stockholm: FOI, 2005).
Uffe Ellemann-Jensen, *Fodfejl* (Copenhagen: Gyldendal, 2004).
Ib Faurby, *NATO efter det kalla kriget* (Stockholm: Ministry of Defence, 1998).
Finlands säkerhets-och försvarspolitik 2004. Statsrådets redogörelse SR 6/2004 (Helsinki: Statsrådets kanslis publikationsserie 17/2004).
Gregory Flynn (ed.), *NATO's Northern Allies. The National Security Policies of Belgium, Denmark, the Netherlands, and Norway* (Totowa, New Jersey: Rowman & Allanheld, 1985).
—, "The United States, the Changing Europe, and the Nordic Region," in Martin O. Heisler (ed.), *The Nordic Region: Changing Perspectives in International Relations* (The Annals of the American Academy of Political and Social Science, November 1990).
Lars Peter Fredén, *Förvandlingar. Baltikums frigörelse och svensk diplomati 1989-1991* (Stockholm: Atlantis, 2004).
—, *Återkomsten. Svensk säkerhetspolitik och de baltiska ländernas första år i självständighet 1991-1994* (Stockholm: Atlantis, 2006).

John Lewis Gaddis, *Strategies of Containment: A Critical Appraisal of Postwar American National Security Policy* (New York: Oxford University Press, 1982).
Carl-Axel Gemzell, "Warszawapakten, DDR och Danmark: kampen för en maritim operationsplan," *Historisk Tidskrift* (Copenhagen), 1996.
—, "Warszawapaktens militära planering mot Danmark," paper, 1998.
Grønland under den kolde krig: dansk og amerikansk sikkerhedspolitik 1945-1968 (Copenhagen: DUPI, 1997).
Birthe Hansen (ed.), *European Security - 2000* (Copenhagen: Copenhagen Political Studies Press, 1995).
— (ed.) *Good Cop, Bad Cop. Transatlantic Challenges* (Copenhagen: DIIS, 2003).
Martin O. Heisler (ed.), *The Nordic Region: Changing Perspectives in International Relations* (The Annals of the American Academy of Political and Social Science, November 1990).
Bertel Heurlin, *Verden 2000. Teorier og tendenser i international politik* (Copenhagen, Gyldendal, 1996).
—, "Denmark and the Baltic Sea. Three minor articles," DUPI, *Working Papers* 1997/9.
—, "NATO, Security and the Baltic States. A New World, a New Security, a New NATO," DUPI, *Working Papers* 1997/10.
—, "Explaining European Integration: The Role of the United States," DUPI, *Working Papers* 1998/16.
Bertel Heurlin and Hans Mouritzen (eds.), *Danish Foreign Policy Yearbook 1999* (Copenhagen: DUPI, 1999).
Bertel Heurlin and Sten Rynning (eds.), *Det 21. århundredes trusler* (Copenhagen: DIIS, 2006).
Kjeld Hillingsø, *Trusselsbilledet - en koldkriger taler ud* (Copenhagen: Gyldendal, 2004).

Hans-Henrik Holm, "The Rise and Decline of Foreign Policy Activism: The Case of Denmark" in Ann-Sofie Dahl (Nilsson) and Norman Hillmer (eds.), *Activism and (non)alignment* (Stockholm: Swedish Institute for International Affairs, 2002).

Karoliina Honkanen, *The Influence of Small States on NATO Decision-Making. The Membership Experiences of Denmark, Norway, Hungary and the Czech Republic* (Stockholm: FOI, 2002a).

—, "Small States in NATO Decision-Making: Influence or Accommodation?" in Ann-Sofie Dahl and Norman Hillmer (eds.), *Activism and (non)alignment* (Stockholm: Swedish Institute for International Affairs, 2002b).

Bo Huldt and Gunilla Herolf (eds.), *Towards a New European Security Order* (Stockholm: Swedish Institute for International Affairs, Yearbook 1990–91).

Bo Huldt and Ulrika Johannessen (eds.), *1st Annual Stockholm Conference on Baltic Sea Security and Cooperation* (Stockholm: Swedish Institute for International Affairs, 1997).

Bo Huldt, Sven Rudberg and Elisabeth Davidson, *The Transatlantic Link* (Stockholm: Swedish National Deefense College, 2001).

Douglas Hurd, *Alistair Buchan Memorial Lecture* (London: IISS, March 28, 1996)

Hans Hækkerup, "Cooperation around the Baltic Sea: Danish perspectives and initiatives," *NATO Review*, May 1995.

Efraim Inbar and Gabriel Scheffer (eds.), *The National Security of Small States in a Changing World* (London: Frank Cass, 1997).

Max Jakobson, "Europas säkerhetspolitik vid vägskälet," *Internationella Studier* No. 2, Summer 1996.

—, *Finland in the New Europe* (Washington: CSIS, The Washington Papers/175, 1998).

Albert Jónsson, *Iceland, NATO and the Keflavik Base* (Reyjkavik: The Icelandic Commission on Security and International Affairs, 1989).

Pauli Järvenpää, "Finland: An Image of Continuity in Turbulent Europe," in Martin O. Heisler (ed.), *The Nordic Region: Changing Perspectives in International Relations* (The Annals of the American Academy of Political and Social Science, November 1990)

—, "GUSP och Finland – utvecklingen av militär krishanteringskapacitet", in Pauli Järvenpää, Kirsti Kauppi et al., *Finlands plats i världen? EU:s utrikes- och säkerhetspolitik* (Helsinki: Foreign Ministry, 2003a).

Pauli Järvenpää, Kirsti Kauppi et al., *Finlands plats i världen? EU:s utrikes- och säkerhetspolitik* (Helsinki: Foreign Ministry, 2003b).

Birgit Karlsson, *Handelspolitik eller politisk handling – Sveriges handel med öststaterna 1946–1952.* (Göteborg: Göteborgs universitet, 1992).

Efraim Karsh, "Geographical Determinism: Finnish Neutrality Revisited", *Cooperation & Conflict*, Vol. XXI, 1986.

Rodney Kennedy-Minott, *Lonely Path to Follow. Nonaligned Sweden, United States/NATO, and the USSR* (Stanford: Stanford University, Hoover Institution 1990).

Edward Killham, *The Nordic Way*, (Washington, D.C.: The Compass Press, 1993).

Olav F. Knudsen, "Of Lambs and Lions: Relations Between Great Powers and their Smaller Neighbors," *Cooperation and Conflict*, Vol. XXIII, 1988.

—, "Norway: Domestically Driven Foreign Policy," in Martin O.

Heisler (ed.), *The Nordic Region: Changing Perspectives in International Relations* (The Annals of the American Academy of Political and Social Science, November 1990).

—, (ed.), *Stability and Security in the Baltic Sea Region* (London: Frank Cass Publishers, 1999).

Olav F. Knudsen & Iver B. Neumann, *Subregional Security Cooperation in the Baltic Sea Area. An Exploratory Study* (Oslo: Norwegian Institute of International Affairs, NUPI Report, No. 189, March 1995).

Olof Kronvall, *Den bräckliga barriären: Finland i svensk säkerhetspolitik 1948–1962* (Stockholm: Stockholms universitet, 2003).

Joseph Kruzich and Anna Fahraeus, *2nd Annual Stockholm Conference on Baltic Security and Cooperation. Towards an Inclusive Security Structure in the Baltic Sea Region* (Stockholm: US Embassy, 1997).

Joseph Kruzich and Madeleine Kornfehl (eds.), *Baltic Sea Region Brief* (Stockholm: US Embassy, 1998).

Joseph Kruzich and Anna Fahraeus (eds.), *Speeches by Lyndon l. Olsen, Jr, Ambassador of the United States of America to Sweden, 1998–1999* (Stockholm: US Embassy, 1999).

F. Stephen Larrabee, "NATO, The EU and Russia in the 21st Century: Strategic Challenges and Dilemmas." Paper, Spring, 2001.

Leif Leifland, *Frostens år* (Stockholm: Nerenius & Santérus, 1997).

Lessons Learned From the BALTAP Project (Copenhagen: Ministry of Defence, January, 2001).

Robert J. Lieber, *No Common Power* (New York: HarperCollins College Publishers, 1995).

— (ed.), *Eagle Adrift. American Foreign Policy at the End of the Century* (New York: Longman, 1997).

—, *Eagle Rules? Foreign Policy and American Primacy in the 21st Century.* (New York: Prentice Hall, 2002).

—, *The American Era. Power and Strategy For the 21st Century* (New York: Cambridge University Press, 2005).

Henrik Liljegren, *Från Tallinn till Turkiet – som svensk och diplomat* (Stockholm: Timbro, 2004).

Geir Lundestad, *America, Scandinavia, and the Cold War* (Oslo: Universitetsforlaget, 1980).

Lloyd J. Matthews (ed.), *The Future of the American Military Presence in Europe* (Washington, DC: The Strategic Studies Institute, 2000).

Ernest R. May, "National Security in American History," in Graham Allison and Gregory F. Treverton (eds.), *Rethinking America's Security. Beyond Cold War to New World Order* (New York: W.W Norton & Company, 1992).

Steven E. Miller, "Nordic Security in a Europe without the United States," in Martin O. Heisler (ed.), *The Nordic Region: Changing Perspectives in International Relations* (The Annals of the American Academy of Political and Social Science, November 1990a).

—, "US withdrawal and NATO's Northern Flank: Impact and Implications," in Jane M.O. Sharp (ed.), *Europe after an American Withdrawal. Economic and Military Issues* (Stockolm: SIPRI and Oxford University Press, 1990b)

—, "The Superpowers and Nordic Security in Post-Cold War Europe," in Bo Huldt and Gunilla Herolf (eds.), *Towards a New European Security Order* (Stockholm: Swedish Institute for International Affairs, Yearbook 1990–91).

Simon Moores, "'Neutral on our Side': US Policy towards Sweden during the Eisenhower Administration," *Cold War History*, No. 3, 2002.

Hans Mouritzen, "Tension between the Strong, and the Strategies of the Weak," *Journal of Peace Research*, Vol. 28, No. 2, 1991.

—, *Three Nordic Reactions to the Soviet Coup and Disintegration 1991: testing Weak Power Theory*, (Copenhagen: Centre for Peace and Conflict Research, Working Papers 13/1992).

—, *Europas fremtid – et euro-atlantisk geopolitisk puslespil* (Copenhagen: DIIS, 2005).

Kenneth A. Myers, *North Atlantic Security: The Forgotten Flank?* (The Washington Papers, Vol. VI, 1979).

Torbjörn Nilsson (ed.), *Anfall eller försvar. Högern i svensk politik under 1900-talet* (Stockholm: Santérus, 2002).

Thorsten Borring Olesen and Poul Villaume, *I blokopdelingens tegn: 1945–1972* (Copenhagen: Dansk udenrigspolitisk historie, volume 5, 2005).

"Om kriget kommit. Förberedelser för mottagande av militärt bistånd 1949-1969," (Stockholm: *SOU* 1994:11) In English as *Had there been war*.

Bo Petersson, *Med Moskvas ögon* (Stockholm: Arena, 1994).

Nikolaj Petersen, *Denmark and NATO 1949–1987* (Oslo: Forsvarsstudier 2/1987).

—, "Denmark's Foreign Relations in the 1990," in Martin O. Heisler (ed.), *The Nordic Region: Changing Perspectives in International Relations* (The Annals of the American Academy of Political and Social Science, November 1990).

Tomas Ries, *The Nordic Dilemma in the 80s: Maintaining Regional Stability under New Strategic Conditions* (Geneva: PSIS Occasional Papers, No. 1, July 1982)

—, "Developments in East-West Security and Northern Europe," in Ciro Elliot Zoppo (ed.), *Nordic Security at the Turn of the Twenty-First Century* (New York: Greenwood Press, 1992).

—, *Finland and NATO* (Helsinki: National Defence College, 1999).

—, "The Atlantic Link: A View From Finland," in Bo Huldt, Sven Rudberg and Elisabeth Davidson, *The Transatlantic Link* (Stockholm: Swedish National Defense College, 2001).

—, "Activism and Nonalignment," in Ann-Sofie Dahl and Norman Hillmer (eds.), *Activism and (non)alignment* (Stockholm: Swedish Institute for International Affairs, 2002).

Olav Riste, "'Janus Septentrionalis'? The Two Faces of Nordic Non-Alignment," *The History of Neutrality*, Finnish Historical Society 1993.

Gustav Schmidt (ed.), *A History of NATO. The First Fifty Years* (London: Palgrave, 2001).

Simon Serfaty, *Stay the Course. European Unity and Atlantic Solidarity* (Washington, DC: The Washington Papers/171, 1997).

Jane M.O. Sharp (ed.), *Europe after an American Withdrawal. Economic and Military Issues* (Stockolm: SIPRI and Oxford University Press, 1990).

Charles Silva, *Keep Them Strong, Keep Them Friendly. Swedish–American Relations and the Pax Americana, 1948–1952* (Stockholm: Stockholm University, 1999).

Kjertil Skogrand and Rolf Tamnes, *Fryktens likevekt. Atombomben, Norge og verden 1945–1970.* (Oslo: Tiden, 2001).

Stanley R. Sloan, "Global Burdensharing in the Post-Cold War World", *CRS Report for Congress*,

October 8, 1993, (Washington, DC: The Library of Congress).

Keith C. Smith, *Baltic-Russian Relations: Implications for European Security* (Washington, DC: CSIS, 2002).

Mark Smith, *NATO Enlargement during the Cold War: Strategy and System in the Western Alliance* (New York: Palgrave, 2000).

Gerald B. Solomon, *The NATO enlargement Debate, 1990–1997. Blessings of Liberty* (Washington, DC: The Washington Papers/174, Praeger, 1998).

Olafur Stephensen, "The Trans-Atlantic Link Secured," *Scandinavian Review*, September, 1996.

Rolf Tamnes, *The United States and the Cold War in the High North* (Oslo: Ad Notam forlag As, 1991).

—, *Oljealder 1965–1995*. (Oslo: Norsk Utenrikspolitikks Historie, bind 6. Universitetsforlaget, 1997).

—, "The Strategic Importance of the High North during the Cold War," in Gustav Schmidt (ed.), *A History of NATO. The First Fifty Years* (London: Palgrave, 2001).

Staffan Thorsell, *Sverige i Vita Huset* (Stockholm: Bonnier Fakta, 2004).

Henrik Thune and Ståle Ulriksen, "Prestige and Penance Through Peace –Norway as an Allied Activist" in Ann-Sofie Dahl and Norman Hillmer (eds.), *Activism and (non)alignment* (Stockholm: Swedish Institute for International Affairs, 2002).

Ståle Ulriksen, "Security Complexes, Subsystems and Great Powers. Three notes on the structure of the international system," *NUPI Working papers*, No. 581, August 1997 (Oslo: NUPI, 1997).

Poul Villaume, *Allieret med forbehold. Danmark, NATO og den kolde krig. En studie i dansk sikkerhedspolitik 1949– 1961* (Copenhagen: Eirene, 1995).

—, "Denmark and NATO Through 50 Years," in Bertel Heurlin and Hans Mouritzen (eds.), *Danish Foreign Policy Yearbook 1999* (Copenhagen: DUPI, 1999).

Raimo Väyrunen, "Regional Conflict Formations: An Intractable Problem of International Relations," in *Journal of Peace Research*, Vol. 21, No. 4, 1984.

Kenneth N. Waltz, *Theory of International Politics* (Reading, Mass: Addison-Wesley Publishing Company, 1983)

—, "The United States and the New World Order," in Birthe Hansen (ed.), *European Security – 2000* (Copenhagen: Copenhagen Political Studies Press, 1995)

Ole Wæver, "Nordic Nostalgia: Northern Europe after the Cold War," *International Affairs*, 1992, No. 1.

—, "What is Security? – The Securityness of Security," in Birthe Hansen (ed.), *European Security – 2000* (Copenhagen: Copenhagen Political Studies Press 1995).

Dov S. Zakheim, "The Role of Denmark in the Baltic Sea: An American View," paper, 1997.

—, "The United States and the Nordic Countries During the Cold War," *Nordic Journal of International Studies/ Cooperation and Conflict*, Vol 33, No. 2, June 1998.

Ciro Elliot Zoppo (ed.), *Nordic Security at the Turn of the Twenty-First Century* (New York: Greenwood Press, 1992).

Documents and speeches

1st Annual Stockholm Conference on Baltic Sea Security and Cooperation (Stockholm: Swedish Institute of International Affairs, 1996).

2nd Annual Stockholm Conference on Baltic Security and Cooperation. Towards an Inclusive Security Structure in the Baltic Sea Region (Stockholm: US Embassy, 1997).

A Charter of Partnership Among the United States of America and the Republic of Estonia, Republic of Latvia, and Republic of Lithuania (United States Information Service, January, 1998).

Address by Senator Jesse Helms, "Towards a Compassionate Conservative Foreign Policy", (American Enterprise Institute, January 11, 2001).

American Engagement in the Baltic Sea Region. Speech by Ambassador Lyndon L. Ohlson, Jr., (Conference Organized by the Swedish Atlantic Council, Stockholm, 1998).

Baltic Action Plan (US Mission to NATO, February 1997).

Baltic Sea Region Brief (United States Information Service, Stockholm, 1998).

Documents from NATO Summits at: www.nato.int.

Lecture by Prime Minister Anders Fogh Rasmussen (The George Washington University, Wednesday, 27th of March, 2002).

Remarks by President George W. Bush at University Library (Warsaw, Poland, 16 June, 2001).

The Baltic Sea Region and European Security after Madrid. A Speech by Ambassador Thomas L. Siebert (Swedish Air Force Regiment in Luleå, October 1, 1997).

The Declaration on Euro-Atlantic Security and Cooperation. Issued by Heads of State and Government (Madrid, July 8, 1997).

The New Atlantic Community and the Baltic Sea Region. Speech by Ambassador Thomas L. Siebert, Swedish Atlantic Council and the South Sweden Chamber of Commerce (February 7, 1997).

The New Hanseatic League. Remarks by Deputy Assistant Secretary of State Ronald D. Asmus (Helsinki, October 8, 1997, also in *Baltic Sea Region Brief* (1998).

United States Security Strategy for Europe and NATO (Washington, D.C: Department of Defense, 1995).

Newspapers etc

Berlingske Tidende
Dagens Nyheter
Frankfurter Allgemeine Zeitung
Hufvudstadsbladet
Svenska Dagbladet
The Economist
The International Herald Tribune
The Washington Post
Turun Sanomat
Vårt Försvar

The reader of this book may also be interested in:

Robert Dalsjö

Life-Line Lost

The Rise and Fall of 'Neutral' Sweden's Secret Reserve Option of Wartime Help from the West

Mikael Nilsson

Tools of Hegemony

Military Technology and Swedish-American Security Relations 1945–1962

Marie Demker

Colonial Power and National Identity

Pierre Mendès France and the History of French Decolonization

Read more and buy them from:

www.santerus.se

or ask your local book store

www.ingramcontent.com/pod-product-compliance
Lightning Source LLC
Chambersburg PA
CBHW031635160426
43196CB00006B/427